Video CINEMA

Video CINEMA

Techniques and Projects for
Beginning **Filmmakers**

John Parris Frantz

CHICAGO
REVIEW
PRESS

Library of Congress Cataloging-in-Publication Data

Frantz, John Parris.
Video cinema : techniques and projects for beginning filmmakers /
John Parris Frantz. — 1st ed.
p.   cm.
"A Ziggurat book."
Includes index.
ISBN 1-55652-228-2 : $14.95
I. Title.
PN1992.94.F73   1994
791.43 — dc20   94-25878
CIP

All photographs by John Parris Frantz

First edition

Published by Chicago Review Press, Incorporated
814 North Franklin Street
Chicago, Illinois, 60610

Printed in the United States of America

ISBN: 1-55652-228-2
1 2 3 4 5 6 7 8 9 10

To my parents,
Les and Betty,
who emphasized education

CONTENTS

Acknowledgments

Thank you, Dr. Seymour Miller, a great educator who showed me how video is potentially a great educational tool. And the dozens of magazine editors I've worked with for the last fifteen years who helped make me a better writer and educator.

Preface

I know this sounds corny, but there really isn't anything more exciting than a movie set at the moment when the director shouts "Lights . . . camera . . . action!"

I know there are thousands of aspiring young movie directors waiting to yell those words and display their filmmaking aptitude. Too many are stifled, however, because they lack technical knowledge, motivation, or equipment.

I also know there are thousands of camcorders, probably hundreds of thousands of dollars' worth, sitting idly in boxes. They collect dust between their occasional appearances at birthday parties and weddings.

This book intends to get those inactive camcorders into the hands of those aspiring filmmakers. I can't turn you into a filmmaker, but I hope to give you the tools you need to start turning yourself into one.

Fortunately, a few decades ago, young Steven Spielberg wasn't stifled. While his peers played sports and were busy with social activities, Spielberg was hard at work making amateur movies. His early projects nurtured a developing talent that subsequently produced *Jaws*, *Raiders of the Lost Ark*, *Jurassic Park*, and *Schindler's List*.

The art of making videos involves more than pushing the record button on a camcorder. It draws on all the arts. Writing scripts and storyboards requires a flair with words. Animation often depends on a talent for drawing and using color. Music, a foundation for many videos, demands an understanding of the interplay between music and images. Persuasive speech is important in documentaries and commercials, which use narration and interviews.

Videomaking allows you to display your own strengths. All the arts are usually present, but traditional art skills are not required. Videographers can grasp underlying concepts of art—composition, balance, color—through a camcorder viewfinder; they don't even have to be able to draw a straight line. The camcorder thus becomes a liberating artist's tool, a way to work creatively with what already exists and can be made visually interesting; a videographer doesn't have to confront a blank canvas or a lump of clay. The pleasure—the creativity itself—lies in the presentation of real objects and people. Even animation can be wonderful when two- or three-dimensional objects are used instead of drawings.

Some chapters in this book are simply fun projects. Take the video letter chapter. Anyone can make and send a video letter for the personal and social entertainment of communicating with a friend or relative on a TV screen. The video yearbook chapter is intended to be both fun and functional, because it tells you how to create something you and your friends can enjoy and treasure for years. Likewise, "The Art of the Interview" will help you develop good interviewing skills as well as encourage you to document the lives of your grandparents for a video that promises to be valued by your entire family. Yet the most stimulating chapters probably are those that invite you to write a script, position the camera in unexpected ways, enlighten an audience, or, perhaps most difficult of all, make people laugh.

Whether you are as comfortable looking through a viewfinder as you are looking through your own eyes, or you have just opened the box and removed the camcorder for the first time, this book can take you as far as your imagination and dedication will allow. Are you a future Steven Spielberg? You'll never know until you get started, until you advance from operating a video camera to the greater challenge of making effective videos.

How to Operate Your Camcorder

This chapter is for those of you who are unfamiliar with operating your camcorder—those who take off the camcorder's lens cap, push the red record button, and find that nothing happens. If your camcorder is working fine and you're confident you know how to operate it, turn to the next chapter and get started.

Power is, of course, essential. All camcorders need power to operate. Power can come from a wall outlet (AC power) or from a nicad battery (DC power), but it has to come from somewhere.

All camcorders come with a battery, but the battery on your camcorder might need charging. Find the battery charger (which in most cases doubles as the AC power cord) and charge the battery. If after a couple of hours of charging, the battery still doesn't power the camcorder (make sure you turn the camcorder on!), you may need to replace the battery. Batteries wear out or fail because of underuse or because they are not charged regularly. If you've given up on the battery, try hooking up the AC power attachment by following the directions in the camcorder's operating manual.

Another reason why your camcorder might not be operating properly is an empty tape transport. A camcorder won't operate without a video-tape.

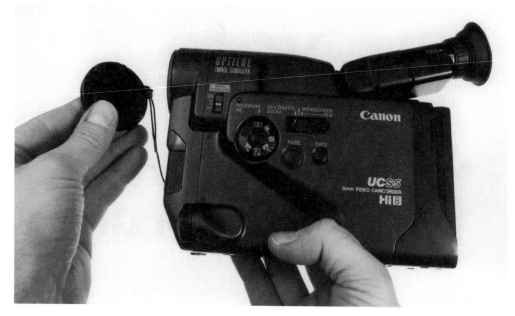

Photographers and cinematographers often joke about forgetting to take off the lens cap, but it isn't funny when it happens. In fact, many professionals sometimes forget this fundamental step.

Another factor is the safety tab, which is a feature on all videocassettes. On some tapes it resembles a tiny square cutout on the thin side of the cassette. The safety tab is connected to the cassette itself only on one side. The other three sides of the square are separated from the cassette shell. If it's connected to the cassette, you'll be able to record. If someone has pulled it out and removed it, the cassette will not allow you to record because the void of a missing safety tab triggers the camcorder out of record mode. If the safety tab is indeed missing, some adhesive tape placed over the square will allow you to record on the cassette. On other types of tapes the safety tab resembles a little red door on the side of the cassette. When the little red door is on one side, you can record on the cassette tape; when the door is on the other, you can't.

The purpose of the safety tab is to protect something you've recorded. If you've recorded something worth saving and you don't want to erase it accidentally or record over it in the future, you have the option of disabling the tape to prevent any future recordings. Just slide the little red door over, or, for the other style of tape, just remove the tab.

Another thing to check is the dew indicator. You should see some type of little picture in the viewfinder (the tiny screen you look into to see what

It may sound elementary, but you have to push the record button to start recording. If your camcorder has a hand strap, the record button is probably easy to reach with your thumb. Pictured are two different models. The model on the left has a round record button. The one on the right has an oblong record button.

the camera is recording) of something wet. Your camcorder probably isn't wet inside, but if it's in a high-humidity environment it might be shutting off automatically because of excessive moisture. To solve this problem, place the camcorder in a dry environment with the tape transport open to eliminate the moisture. The problem might be solved in a few minutes or take as long as a day. Some dry environments might be a bedroom with lots of fabrics, such as bedspreads, pillows, and clothes. A not-so-dry environment is a basement or a bathroom. Also, do not at any time put the camcorder in direct sunlight.

One last thing to check is the switch most camcorders have that changes them from cameras to VCRs and vice versa. If your camcorder has this switch and it's on "VCR," your camcorder is ready to play back a tape, not record onto one. Make sure this function switch is turned to "camera."

If you've tried all of these things and are still unsuccessful, ask someone with technical camcorder experience. Your unit might need servicing.

If you can't get the camcorder to record, check the safety tab on the videocassette. On VHS tapes, the safety tab is a plastic slot that can be punched out. In this illustration, the safety tab is pulled up but not broken off. Once the safety tab is punched out, the cassette can be played back but no longer recorded on. If you have a valuable tape that you don't want to record on anymore, be sure to punch out the safety tab. On VHS-C and 8mm tapes, a small, red door on the back of the tape can be closed to prevent accidental recording.

Using the Right Type of Videotape

Another cause of temporary camcorder failure is putting the wrong format of cassette in your camcorder. A camcorder's format is the type of system the camcorder runs on. If you have any computer experience, you know that IBM software won't run on Apple (MacIntosh) equipment and vice versa because they have different, incompatible formats.

Unfortunately, the camcorder world also has two incompatible formats. One is VHS, which is the format for 99 percent of the world's VCRs. When most early camcorders first appeared on the market they used full-sized VHS cassettes (just like the kind that are rented at video stores). After recording, camcorder users could pop their camcorder tapes right into the VCR and play back what they had just recorded. Nearly half of

The three most common video formats. *Back to front:* full-sized VHS cassette, 8mm tape cassette, VHS-C cassette. Your camcorder probably uses one of these three formats.

today's camcorders are VHS; you'll know because you'll see "VHS" on the outside of the unit somewhere.

The competing format to VHS is 8mm. This format was invented to help make camcorders smaller. The 8mm tape cassette isn't much larger than an audio cassette. You'll know if your camcorder uses this format because you'll see "8" or "8mm" on the side of the camcorder. Unfortunately, 8mm tapes can't play on VHS cameras or VCRs.

To offset the popularity of 8mm, VHS camcorder manufacturers came up with their own small format called VHS-C. The "C" stands for compact, as the videocassettes are about the same size as 8mm, but a little thicker. Once again, VHS-C tapes won't work in 8mm camcorders. Although VHS-C cassettes have the compatible VHS format of home VCR decks, they are too small to fit into the home VCR deck and thus need an adaptor. The adaptor is a full-sized VHS case that is empty inside. The VHS-C cassettes are placed inside this VHS cassette shell to play in conventional VCR home decks. To further complicate matters, the manufacturers of

The three formats and their increased resolution counterparts are VHS/Super-VHS, 8mm/Hi-8mm, and VHS-C/Super-VHS-C (not pictured). *Clockwise from left:* VHS-C, VHS, Super-VHS, 8mm, Hi-8mm.

VHS and 8mm tried even more one-upmanship. They both invented their own versions of another format that are based on the existing formats but offer better resolution. The 8mm version is called "Hi-8mm," and the VHS version is called "Super-VHS" or "S-VHS." So now there are four types of camcorders. Your camcorder is a VHS, 8mm, S-VHS, or Hi-8mm model. Make sure the videocassette you use is the same format as your camcorder, or you may not be able to record properly.

Remember that most camcorders actually have a VCR inside of them, which allows them to play back. Try to eliminate the need of playing your camcorder tape through your home VCR deck and TV. Instead, hook up your camcorder directly to the TV to play back your tapes. Your camcorder owner's manual will explain what cords, plugs, and connections you need and how to set it up.

Checklist

Here's a helpful checklist to get your camcorder running and recording. The hints you just read are mentioned here only briefly. If you don't understand them, go back to the beginning of this chapter and read the instructions again.

1. Is the battery charged and installed on the camcorder?
2. If using AC power, is the cord plugged in?
3. Is the power button on?
4. Is the lens cap off?
5. Have you pressed the red recording button?
6. Do you see anything in the viewfinder, such as the dew indicator, to denote a problem?
7. Is your videocassette's format the same as your camcorder's?
8. Are you inserting the cassette properly?
9. Is the safety tab still on the cassette or is the red door in the correct position?

Here are some additional tips if the recording isn't up to the quality you expect.

1. Make sure the lens is clean.
2. Make sure the camcorder is running on automatic focus.
3. When playing your cassette on the TV, make sure that the TV is set to the same channel frequency as the camcorder (channel 3 or 4).

Now it's time for the fun part. Go on to the next chapters and start videotaping.

2

A Point-and-Shoot Exercise

The first and most important step toward thinking and seeing like a filmmaker is deciding where you are going to put (or where you should stand and hold) the camera. You know the basics of camcorder operation. Now it's time to advance from simply using a videocamera to becoming a videographer.

Our first project is an easy point-and-shoot exercise. Point-and-shoot means exactly what it says: point the camcorder at something and videotape it. This project will be quick and easy because you're not going to get bogged down with trying to use all the many controls and gadgets on your camcorder.

First you need a subject. It can be anything, but it's best to pick an interesting activity happening around your house or neighborhood. The only requirement is that the activity be at least two minutes long. But remember, two minutes goes by much faster than you think, so almost no activity is too brief. If you can't think of a subject, here are five ideas for subjects you might find somewhere near your house.

■ That noisy garage band next door or local music group with all those great guitar licks.

Get your camcorder out and capture some video, no matter what it is. You can't get better at making videos unless you start shooting. You need to be comfortable with your camera.

- A neighbor's or family member's interesting or unusual hobby, such as repairing classic cars or collecting baseball cards.
- A community event, such as a parade, orchestra concert, or street festival.
- A sporting event is a great idea, too. A soccer, football, baseball, or basketball game or any other sports event with lots of action will work. It doesn't have to be a professional game; it simply can be your friends playing at the nearest park.
- Even something less exciting, such as someone painting a house or washing a car, can work.

Let's use the parade as our subject example. Don't worry if you can't find a parade, the skills we're going to learn apply equally to filming other subjects.

Since you're going "on location," you've got to be portable. In other words, make sure you've got at least one fully charged battery, because there aren't any electrical outlets to plug into at a parade.

Check your owner's manual to determine how long your battery will last. Usually manufacturers include in the camcorder kit an inexpensive battery that only lasts twenty minutes. You might want to buy one or two more batteries at a camcorder store, but we won't be videotaping more than twenty minutes at a time in the first few projects.

Making the Best Use of the Sun

Once you've arrived at the parade site with a charged battery, camcorder, and cassette, the position of the sun will determine where you stand. Frontlighting (having the sun or any other light source behind you) is best. Second choice is having the sun above you. The sun will be above you sometime between 10:30 A.M. and 2:30 P.M. It is best if you can position yourself with the sun at your back or above you. You don't want to have the sun in front of you and behind the subject. This positioning is called backlighting, as the sun lights the backs of the subjects. When backlit, the front of your subject will appear very dark with little detail. Obviously you want the complete opposite; you want the front of the subject to be well lit and the background darker. Some camcorders have a backlight function that lightens the subject when light is pouring in toward the camcorder, but it is at the expense of the background, which becomes washed out and overexposed. Aside from the problems of backlighting, pointing your camcorder toward the sun is still not recommended because the bright light can damage the camcorder's sensitive insides.

Think carefully about your camera position. Stand where the light is good and the view is interesting. When you've found a good view without obstruction and a position that allows the sun to light your subjects properly, point and shoot.

Backlighting or videotaping with the sun shining over the subject's shoulder and toward the camera separates the subject from the background through the halo light effect on the hair. A disadvantage of backlighting, however, is the way it darkens the subject's face. Because the camcorder automatically adjusts its exposure for the bright background, it allows less light to expose the scene. Meanwhile, the subject's face, which is considerably darker than the background because it's facing away from the sun, appears even darker in the process.

You can compensate for backlighting by adding a white reflector card (white posterboard at least 2 feet by 2 feet). Place the reflector card slightly underneath the subject's face to allow the sun to bounce off the card and illuminate your subject's face naturally. Notice the effect of the card under the chin. In this example, however, the subject still has shadowing under the eyes.

Another method of filling in light on the subject's face is to use a video light. Notice how evenly lit the face of the subject appears. However, this example lacks the contrast of the shadows in the previous photo.

With frontlighting where the sun is shining over the shoulder of the camcorder operator, there isn't the three-dimensional effect of backlighting. It's rather flat looking, and the hair isn't highlighted as much. However, unless you're skilled with backlighting and filling in shadows, frontlighting is preferred, since it is easier to obtain good-quality video by using this method.

Here are examples of a long shot and a medium shot. A close-up shot appears on the next page.

Using the Camcorder Functions to Your Advantage

You'll notice your camcorder has a zoom lens, which allows you to zoom in close to your subject or zoom out and put the subject far away in the distance. Somewhere on your camcorder there's a button with a "W" and a "T" on it. These letters stand for wide angle and telephoto. Press the "W," and you'll see the viewfinder capture more of the subject. Press the "T," on the other hand, and you'll see the subject move closer to you with less area around it.

To begin our production, press "W" until it stops moving, and videotape something big like a marching band or a parade float. This is called a long shot. The subject is far away, and you can see much of the activity around it.

Next let's get a closer shot by videotaping just four or five people in the marching band or just the float itself with nothing else around it. This is called a medium shot.

Finally let's move in even closer to the face of one person in the marching band or riding on a float. This is called a close-up.

Each of these shots should be at least thirty seconds long. Try filming some other subjects at the event. Remember, you don't always have to shoot people in the parade. Try finding someone across the street pointing at a float, or maybe a little boy standing in awe as a clown comes near him. The spectators can be just as interesting on film as the participants.

While you're practicing all of your long, medium, and close-up shots, you'll notice the lens mechanically turning back and forth. Newer camcorders now focus electronically, or inside the unit. You won't see any moving parts, but you will see the picture become slowly focused. Most newer camcorders have an automatic-focus function that focuses the picture for you while you're busy pointing and shooting. Because the parade moves quickly, you'll see the picture slowly become focused. The camcorder is keeping the subject in focus all by itself.

The problem with automatic focusing, however, is that the lens may not be quick enough to focus on fast-moving subjects, resulting in an out-of-focus picture. Focusing manually will solve this problem (read your owner's manual to find the manual mode or manual focus button). When in the manual mode the camcorder no longer focuses automatically; you must focus the lens by hand (manually).

Focusing manually takes practice, and there's no better time to practice than when a float is moving toward you in a parade. Put the lens in a close-up mode by pressing the telephoto button. Position the camcorder on someone standing still a good distance down the street (about forty yards away) in the direction from which the parade is coming. Focus on that person standing still. Now position the camcorder on a marching band member as she marches near to that person. The marching band member should be in focus, too, but not for long. As she marches toward you, she'll get fuzzy and blurry, because the camera is no longer focusing automatically for you. But you can focus manually by slowly turning the outside ring on your lens clockwise as the subject comes toward you until the image is clear. Focusing this way will take a little practice, but you should master it after a few attempts. Now try the opposite. As the marching band member marches away from you, turn your focus ring counterclockwise to keep her in focus.

Tips on Getting the Best Shots

To put finishing touches on this first project, look for some additional interesting items and take close-ups of them. Remember, anything to do with the parade is part of the subject and possibly worth getting on

Get familiar with your zoom function, usually labeled W/T. W stands for wide angle, which is the focal length in this illustration.

videotape. Film a baton twirler's complete routine. Look for a marching band member that's out of step and feature just his feet in the frame. Is there an unusual emblem on a marching band uniform you can get a close-up of? Sometimes floats are made of thousands of flowers. Since there are so many flowers, however, you don't notice each one but instead see the total picture, so try zooming in on one single flower in a float. What kind of food are people eating? Videotape a child eating an ice-cream cone. There are hundreds of items you can zoom in on and feature.

Once you have several minutes of the parade on videotape, you're done with your first camcorder project. Go home and play it on a television screen and examine your work. Is it in focus? Is the camera work steady or does the picture jump around because you didn't hold the camera still?

Chances are, your picture isn't very steady if you held the camcorder in your hand instead of using a tripod. A tripod is a three-legged stand that supports the camcorder steadily. I've seen amateur videos that were so shaky I started to get seasick. If you want to make a videotape that everyone can enjoy, you must keep your camcorder steady.

Tripods are indispensable for steady, professional-looking videos.

T stands for telephoto. This is the same illustration as on page 18, but in a telephoto position. It's best to use a wide-angle shot to establish a scene. Page 18 shows the viewer a football game in a small stadium with a school in the background. Meanwhile, this example gives the viewer a closer look at the action.

In addition to the importance of holding the camcorder steady, there is another important lesson to learn from this project: the value of the close-up. Those long and medium shots are nice, but the viewer wants to see close-ups of objects, such as the musical instruments, and of people, such as the marching band members' faces. The viewer wants to break the barrier of physical and mental distance. Of course not everything should be filmed close up. Long and medium shots add variety, but make sure you give the viewer a lot of close-ups in future productions.

If you didn't choose a parade for your first project, make sure you try the techniques outlined in this chapter on whatever you did choose, whether it's a baseball game, garage band, neighbor's hobby, or any other subject.

As you review your videotape, you undoubtedly will notice that it doesn't compare to professional productions you've seen on television. In fact, it may be downright boring. Don't worry about this difference and go on to the next chapter. It's time to make a more professional-looking video, one that will communicate interesting information in interesting ways.

3

Video Letters

Everyone likes to receive personal letters—carefully crafted messages of friendship including important information about the writer's life. Traditionally, letters have been more revealing and interesting than the means we use today: the quick communication of a phone call, fax machine, or computer network. True letters are more contemplative and creative. Unfortunately, it seems that they are becoming obsolete. But why not take the qualities of a letter and bring them to the the video camera? All you really need to make a video letter is a camcorder, video-tape, and yourself.

The first thing you should do for your video letter is to pick some subjects you would like to talk about. Remember to include as many things as you can that are of common interest to you and your friend. For example, your friend may not care much about hearing that Uncle Horace broke a leg, especially since he doesn't know your Uncle Horace. However, if your friend and Uncle Horace played football together in the backyard at your parent's last party, it might be worth including. Think about what you want to tell your friend, and remember to inquire about his life.

Try to find five to ten subjects to talk about. Then list them in an outline like this:

1. Coming home from a vacation
2. How Uncle Horace broke his leg
3. A new joke or two
4. A book you've just finished reading or a concert you attended
5. Some recent artwork you've done
6. Excerpts from a recent sports event you participated in
7. Ideas about what you want to do in the future

Also think about what will work well on videotape; try to find subjects that can be presented visually. New or active things, like a new building in town, a new car, or a soccer game, are visually interesting and go well with descriptive dialogue.

Items in motion are especially visual. After all, you *are* making a motion picture of sorts. Mountain bike riding, dogs catching frisbees in flight, or a pick-up basketball game are just a few ideas. Remember, coming home from a vacation or Uncle Horace's broken leg will be visually dull unless, of course, you have beach footage or film of poor old Uncle Horace hobbling around in a cast.

Choosing and Lighting the Location

Choose a location in your house that will serve as a video studio. Your bedroom might be nice, especially if you have a blank wall. Position a stool or a small chair with a low back about three feet from the wall. Then take some type of portable spotlight, place it on the floor, and shine the center of the beam on the wall at about the height where your neck would be if you were sitting on the stool right next to the wall. This lighting will produce a plain bright background that gradually darkens toward the top of your head—just like the lighting in a television newscast. Make sure the main room light doesn't overpower the spotlight. You might want to dim it. If you have to turn the main light off, you probably will need to shine either a video light (a quartz halogen light made especially for use in video and film) or a spotlight on your face.

Here's a lighting setup similar to what the professionals use, only these lights are inexpensive clip lights you can buy from a hardware store. The two lights in the foreground evenly light the subject. You can't see the light behind the subject, but you can see its effect of separating the subject from the backdrop.

Here's a lighting effect you can use for a horror story. Simply aim one light up toward the subject's face.

When the light comes only from the right side, the left side of the subject's face will appear dark.

Here's the perfect lighting setup for the video letter. A light behind the subject washes the wall with light. There are also lights shining in front of the subject from the right and the left. Notice the sheen on the hair? That's yet another light above the subject. That's a total of four lights.

You can get really fancy by using a hair light. This is another type of spotlight, which is out of view of the camera, that highlights the crown (the back of your head at the top) of your head. This light makes you look more three-dimensional because it outlines your head and separates it more distinctly from the background. Turn on the television news and look at the newscaster's head. Chances are you will see a shine on the hair of dark-haired people. This effect is produced by a hair light.

Of course neither light is necessary to make a video letter; however, these effects are not only fun to do but they also help make a more professional-looking video.

You've taken an hour to set up lights, prepare an outline, and find a good sitting position on the stool, but you can't get started filming until you aim the camera at your face. And you can't aim the camera until you have a tripod to hold it. If you don't have a tripod, stack up some phone books, or a box on a stool, to construct a platform for the camera. Make it sturdy, though, because you don't want an expensive camcorder falling on the floor. You might want to use masking tape to secure the camcorder and phone books to the stool.

Many camcorders have an external microphone jack. Once you plug in the external microphone, the on-camera microphone is canceled out on most camcorder models. The external microphone allows you to pick up audio closer to the subject without moving the camcorder.

Once the lighting is set and the camcorder is steadied on a tripod or stand, the camera angles should be chosen. First set up a medium shot showing you from your chest or waist to your head. Then, after establishing the scene and introducing yourself and the project's intentions, quickly zoom in for a close-up. Since you're in front of the camera, not behind it and within reach of the zoom lens button, you will need either a friend's help or, if your camcorder offers one, a remote control.

Getting the Best Sound

The audio is as important as the video in the video letter because, without it, the recipient won't hear your message. Make sure the on-camera microphone is plugged in and working. If you want better audio, use an external microphone and place it as close to your mouth as possible (but out of view of the camcorder). Be sure to plug in the external microphone in the camcorder's external microphone jack—most camcorders have

Most external microphone jacks on camcorders accept mini-plugs. Microphones that have a 1/4-inch phone jack or an XLR plug will need an adaptor, and possibly a transformer, to plug into the external microphone jack of a camcorder. The microphone in this example has a 1/4-inch jack, which was adapted with the silver adaptor plug to fit into the mini-plug jack of this camcorder.

them, and usually they're labeled "ext. mic." The input for the external microphone is usually mini-jack size. The microphone you have or borrow from a friend might not fit because many microphones are the larger, headphone-jack size (sometimes called quarter-inch phone jack). This problem is easy to solve. Electronics stores such as Radio Shack sell adaptors for under $3 that will allow the larger phone jack to fit into the smaller mini-jack of your camcorder.

If you aren't using an external microphone of any kind, you should make your on-camera microphone better by closing the door and making sure that other sounds in the house, such as your brother's stereo, barking dogs, or lawn mowers, can't be heard. Put the camera as close to you and your stool as possible. You will need to adjust the zoom lens to the wide-angle position, but at least the on-camera microphone will be closer to you. If you hear too much echo on your voice, bring some soft fabrics into the room. More blankets, pillows, rugs, and other sound

Here are four plugs you might run into. *Left to right:* XLR (sometimes referred to as a canon plug), 1/4-inch phone jack, RCA plug, mini-jack.

absorbers will deaden the echo in the room. Echo (sometimes called reverberation) can be a fine effect for music, but, in the interest of clarity, it should be limited for speech.

Remember, the closer the microphone is to the subject, the better the audio will be, as you will be picking up less room ambient (the echo of the room caused by the subject's voice bouncing off the walls) and more direct sound from your voice. Many television talk shows use lavaliere microphones, sometimes called lapel microphones because they are about the size of a thimble and can clip on the lapel of a jacket.

You're almost ready to start recording, but first you must decide whether you will talk off the top of your head or use cue cards. Cue cards were common in early television production, and some shows still use them. Print what you want to say in large letters on paper or cardboard that is large enough for you to see three to five feet away. The cue cards need to be somewhere near the camera. Any closer to you and they will appear on the video. Ideally, the cue cards should be as close to the lens as possible so that you are almost looking into the camera as you read them. This technique will cause viewers to think that you are looking at them and not the cards. Since the viewers won't see the cue cards, it will also appear to them that you've memorized everything you're saying. If

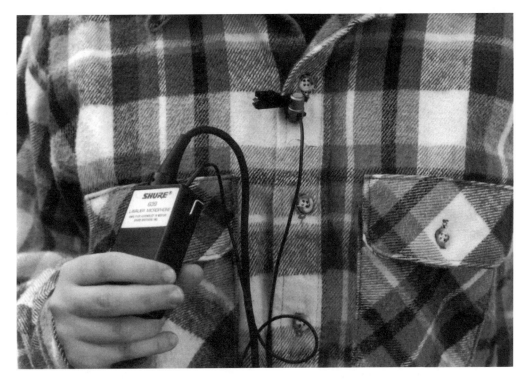

A lavaliere microphone inconspicuously clips to a collar or lapel. Being close to the source—the subject's mouth—eliminates surrounding noise and room echo. The closer the microphone is placed to the source, the better.

you don't think you can improvise (make up) your script as you go along, you might want to write down every word exactly. You also might want to rehearse reading them aloud.

If you can, try to improvise the script rather than read each word; your letter will appear much more natural and conversational that way. The problem with reading cue cards is that, no matter how well you disguise it, your presentation will sound like you're reading something...because you are! If you choose cue cards, don't zoom in too close because it will become even more apparent that you're reading instead of just talking. The closer the camera, the better the viewer can see the subject's eyes move back and forth as he or she reads the cards.

While you are talking during your video letter, look right into the lens as much as possible. When viewers see your tape, they will think you are looking right into their eyes as you're talking. Also remember not to say "ah" or "um," which we typically say when we get stuck on words or can't think of what to say next. Instead of saying "um" after every other word, just pause and say nothing. You'll sound more professional and well rehearsed.

When your cue cards are prepared, the lights are on, the camcorder is ready, and you know what you're going to say, start filming.

Here is a sample of a video letter:

(Camera establishes the entire room setting with a long shot of the subject centered in the middle of the frame. As the subject starts speaking, the camcorder slowly zooms in to a close-up of the subject.)

"It took a lot longer to get home from vacation than it did to get there. It rained most of the time, and at one point it was so fierce we had to pull off the road for an hour. After that, we parked under a viaduct on the interstate because of tornado warnings. So a four-hour ride took about seven hours.

"So after I got home, I had to get ready for school, which started only a few days later. This is the first time I've ever played soccer on a school team, so I've been practicing my skills to make sure I make the team.

"Here is some videotape of our team and yours truly scoring a goal. I'm the guy in the number-nine jersey."

(Pause—get the camcorder ready to receive soccer footage from the soccer tape. Position the camera on yourself again.)

"Do you remember playing football with my Uncle Horace last year? Remember how we were worried he'd break a leg because he was playing like it was the Super Bowl? Well, he made it out of the game unscathed, but he did break his leg a few months later falling down the stairs at his house.

"My art class at school required a watercolor painting the first week of school. I had trouble getting started but decided to paint something from my own imagination rather than trying to copy something real."

(Pause—reposition the camcorder and frame the watercolor painting. Subject speaks while artwork is shown.)

"The assignment was to make a transition from a cool color on the left side of the paper to a group of hot colors on the right side of the paper. I'm still trying to make up my mind about it. What do you think?"

(Pause—reposition the camera back to a headshot and continue the dialogue.)

Making the Duplicate

Once you've finished your video letter, protect your master copy (the videotape on which you recorded your video letter) by snapping off the safety tab in the back of the cassette. (For a reminder about safety tabs see chapter 1.)

Now that your master copy is protected, you are ready to make a duplicate. Never send away a master copy because, if it becomes lost or isn't returned, your hard work is gone forever.

To duplicate your video letter, set up your camcorder next to a VCR. Patch cords should come out of the "video out" and "audio out" of the camcorder and go to the "video in" and "audio in" of the VCR. Some camcorders have a universal output where just one patch cord takes care of the output of both the audio and video signals.

Put your master copy in the camcorder and a blank videocassette in the VCR. Press "play" on the camcorder and "record" on the VCR. If you want to monitor the process, hook up a television to the VCR. You'll be able to watch the duplicate being made. You'll also know when the duplication is over so you can turn off the machines.

If you think your video letter would be interesting to other friends or relatives, make several copies and send one to each person, or ask for your duplicates back so you can send them to other people.

Don't forget two final things in your video letter: say goodbye (or sign off in some interesting way, perhaps by simply moving out of the frame or by fading out on that watercolor painting), and ask the recipient to video a letter back.

A Video Yearbook

Those of you who are interested in making videos that document events will probably enjoy making a video yearbook. With a few adjustments, this project can be adapted for making a video that records an entire year or established period in the life of an individual, a group of friends, a club, or an institution. Not all of you will want to preserve a school year on film, and perhaps many of you will consider school activities too formal or even dull for your creative filmmaking, but this project teaches a lot about working with others and being organized over a long stretch of time—both important aspects of filmmaking. Most important, you can find your own way of documenting a year, regardless of whether you want a formal video, determined by the school's schedule of events, or a more personal one that recalls a year in the life of you and your friends. Many documentaries, which are covered at length in chapter 10, are filmed over the course of several months or a year. Filmmakers often choose to film "A Year in the Life of . . . "

The school yearbook has been around for decades, and the video version is a natural for the nineties. Whether on paper or film, however, the yearbook stems from the perennial desire to capture a year's worth of events, both academic and social. As you become more familiar with film as an art form, you'll see that nostalgia is a recurring theme for filmmakers. Your video yearbook will give you a chance to film people and moments that you suspect will prompt feelings of nostalgia in your audience—and in yourself.

This project should help you to understand that a production schedule that covers an entire year requires a particularly strong commitment. Getting up at 5 A.M. to tape a sports practice or club meeting in September might not seem like much fun anymore come February. And by May you might be out of both energy and film—unless you pace yourself. You have to be organized and yet open to making spontaneous changes in your production plans. You can't predict precisely which events will inspire the best footage and be the most interesting to your audience, nor can you film everyone all the time for an entire year.

The video yearbook includes everything a paper version does, such as faces, groups, and events, but video takes the process one step further: action. Instead of still photos of the prom or a soccer match, the pictures come alive.

This videotape project might not be long in running time, but it will take the entire school year to record. Basically it has three types of videotaping: (1) small and large group shots, (2) interviews with individuals or small groups, and (3) event videotaping.

Probably the first step is getting permission from the principal and/or school board. You could probably do it without permission, but being sanctioned could smooth logistics and help hurdle any unforeseen obstacles hampering your videotaping at an event. For example, at a football game you'll want to get as close to the action as possible, but security might restrict your entry to the sidelines unless you've secured some type of press pass.

What's in a Video Yearbook?

Before you ask permission, write a synopsis, which is an overview or brief outline, of your video yearbook. Here's a sample:

Video Yearbook Synopsis

I. **First week of school**

    A. **Shots of physical changes to the school and notices of new school policies**

B. Long lines of students at registration with candid interviews

II. **Homecoming**
    A. Shots of homecoming pep rally
    B. Highlights of Oct. 12 homecoming football game
       1. Interview with game MVP
       2. Interview with head football coach
    C. **Marching band excerpts (obtain permission to march in formation with the camcorder running?)**
    D. Excerpts of homecoming dance and band
       1. Interviews with homecoming queen and king
       2. Random interviews with dance participants

III. **Fall play**
    A. Excerpts of rehearsals
    B. Interviews with lead actors
    C. Actual performance excerpts
    D. Interview with school newspaper writer reviewing the play

These are just a few of the many events and activities you can include on your video yearbook. It's up to you to know which events to videotape and when and where they take place. One thing is certain, you can't be at every event and videotape everything, so you should consider employing some friends to help you with this project.

Group Portraits

Standard yearbooks usually have pages and pages of group photos. Soccer team, debate club, National Honor Society, orchestra, cheerleading team, etc. You're going to have to make a decision from the onset whether you are making the sort of video yearbook that requires all the groups. Scheduling groups for pictures is time-consuming and very unrewarding. Try teaming up with the paper yearbook staff. They have to photograph all those groups, so maybe you can just tag along when they do so. Let them do all the logistical work.

Regardless, you should know how to shoot a group. It's not as easy as it sounds. The first step in shooting a group is getting them to meet outside. Lighting is much easier outdoors than indoors because it's brighter and more even, so you won't need artificial lights.

Once you organize the group shot and the big day arrives, be sure you're prepared. Make sure your camcorder battery is fully charged. You don't need the hassles of electrical cords, because you're going to be shooting outside with every chance you get.

Let's use the football team picture as an example. Get mentally prepared to be the director. Where will everyone stand or sit? Are teammates supposed to smile at the camera? You need to be prepared because some people will resist being filmed, or worse, being directed. You're going to have your hands full with crowd control.

Although a cloudy day is acceptable, hope for a sunny one. You will need to plan what direction the group must face. There are two directions you don't want to use. You don't want the sun directly behind you, because its intensity will make your subjects squint. And you don't want the sun directly behind the subjects and facing the camcorder, because that will make the camcorder squint. Squint? Well, maybe a piece of hardware is incapable of squinting, but its automatic iris will close down to reduce the exposure on the videotape. When this happens, the camera automatically corrects for the bright sun and not the less-bright subjects in front of the sun (in this case your classmates' faces). The subjects will appear muddy, dark, and underexposed.

Instead of backlighting or frontlighting, the sun should illuminate the group from its right or left. From a side position, the sun lights one side of the group's faces while the other side appears darker with shadows. This adds lighting contrast. I find faces with contrasting light look better than faces equally illuminated with light. The shadows add more dramatic effects.

Using the sun to your best lighting advantage might sound easy, but don't forget you will need an attractive backdrop behind your group as well. Try to find an appealing and colorful natural setting. A group of evergreen trees, or a large blossoming tree, would make an excellent backdrop. If your school is in a concrete jungle, try a plain side of the school as long as the sun is in a good position. Don't place your subjects in front of something white or full of glare. The bright reflections will distract from the main idea—the subjects.

Once you find a site, determine how wide your group can stand in relationship to where the camcorder is positioned. This should be done long before you call everyone to gather outside for the group portrait. Stand at an area in front of the backdrop you selected, look through the camcorder's viewfinder, and determine how wide your group should be positioned in order to stay within the limitations of your focal length. As you're looking through the viewfinder and determining the width of the site, look for some type of land markings on each side of the site. It might be a small bare spot in the grass or a grease spot on the playground. Then put a more visible marking there yourself, such as a small branch or some masking tape. When the group arrives outside for positioning, you can then tell them to stay within the two boundaries you've placed at the site. When you're scouting the site, remember to keep your zoom lens in the wide position, because you're going to need the widest focal area possible.

But once the group is on the site, you've got the challenge of positioning people so that all their faces can be seen. Logically, you'll want to put tall people in the back and shorter people in front. If your class is a typical size, it should be around twenty-five to thirty people. If you're videotaping the football team, which can be quite large in big schools, grandstands and bleachers might be the best choice. You won't have to worry about who's taller, because the different tiers of the bleachers will properly position each team player's face.

But if it's a smaller team, say the basketball team with only twelve players and no bleachers, then place everyone between your markers with taller people in the back and shorter ones in the front.

Videotape the team for approximately one minute. There's not much to do for the audio portion of the tape. You might want each member of the group to state his name and year in school. The audio track might otherwise be littered with complaints, wisecracks, and other comments if you don't control the situation. Remember, in order to get the best audio, you have to position your camcorder (and subsequently the on-camera microphone) as close as possible to the group. That's unless you have an external microphone, which we discussed earlier in this book.

Once you've got one minute of videotape, what do you do next? You could interview several of the stars of the team using techniques outlined in chapter 6, "The Art of the Interview."

Usually people have difficulty improvising to spur-of-the-moment questions. Try to give your questions to the interviewees beforehand so they have a chance to prepare good answers.

Individual Portraits

It was good to videotape the team portrait in direct sunlight, and the interviews will look equally good outdoors—only this time you should use subdued sunlight, such as a shady corner of the school away from traffic and other outdoor noise. A shady area will do one important thing. The lens will open wider to let more light into the camcorder. When that happens, the depth of field will be reduced. When the depth of field is reduced, the background becomes less focused. The subject will stay in focus (as long as you focus the image), and the background will be out of focus (depending on how far back it is from the subject). Additionally, the audio will be better than if you filmed in a large, wide-open space such as an athletic field.

So before you start running around trying to get a better focused background, stop and think about this: We want to concentrate on the subject, and the background only takes our attention away from the subject. The more out of focus and indeterminable the background is, the more attention the viewer will subconsciously place on the subject. So, out of focus is not necessarily bad. However, it isn't desirable for the subject to be out of focus.

Don't forget that the closer you are with the camcorder and the on-camera microphone, the better the audio will be.

Start the interview with the subject stating his or her name. Once you've established the interviewee's name and broken the ice, try asking the featured question, "What's the most exciting thing that happened to you in the last year?" Ask your subject this question while zooming in very closely. Fill the viewfinder with the subject's face and remind them prior to videotaping to respond with their answers while looking directly at the lens.

You'll get plenty of interviewees that won't elaborate on questions, so be a good interviewer and prod them.

Indoor Shooting of Groups or an Individual

If it's a rainy day or too cold outside, you'll have to locate your site indoors. A classroom might be a good site, but you need to make sure it provides enough light for a high-quality video picture. If the low-light indicator flashes in your viewfinder, you might have to bring in extra lights. You can

Depth of field determines how much of the background is in focus and recognizable. If you don't want to take attention away from your main subject, you should strive for a softly focused background. A background in good focus competes with the subject for the viewer's attention.

either use real video lights, or aim some basic clip-on lights at the spot where the class stands. Be sure to place the additional lighting behind the camcorder.

Remember that you'll need plenty of space to film a group portrait, so be sure to move enough desks and chairs out of the portrait area.

The width of the classroom you use might be smaller than the area you planned in the great outdoors, so you might have to transform your two rows into three or four. Once again, the technique of taller people in the back and shorter people in the front will have to be used. One solution is to seat the people in free-standing chairs (not chairs connected to school desks). Seating the first row will allow people in the back rows to be seen better.

If your extra lights are bright enough and you can locate them high in your classroom, bounce or reflect them off the ceiling. A lightly colored wall might also provide diffused lighting. But unless you know someone with quartz halogen lights made especially for video and film, or have a local store that rents them, you're going to have to settle on something simple. If you can't find any clip-on lights, try simple table lamps. Just take the shade off of a lamp and place the lamp behind the camcorder to boost the brightness of the room.

If you're forced to do the interviews indoors too, you'll want to boost that picture quality as well. If your camcorder came with an on-camera light, it wouldn't be bright enough to illuminate the large group, but it will be great for individual interviews. If your camcorder didn't come with an on-camera light, you can buy one at your favorite video store. Or you can use the inexpensive solutions I suggested earlier.

To conclude your video team portraits, you might consider interviewing a school newspaper reporter who can give a synopsis or wrap-up on the team.

In addition to using group portraits and interviews in your video yearbook, you can videotape events. This process is discussed extensively in chapter 2, "A Point-and-Shoot Exercise."

Making Copies

Once you've completed your video yearbook master tape, comprised of the best scenes strung together in a chronological order, it's time to make copies for people who want them. Such copies are called duplicates, and you can make them with several different equipment configurations.

One method is to use your camcorder as the source machine that plays back the master tape. The record machine can be the family VCR, which will hold the receiving tape to be duplicated. (See the "Making the Duplicate" section in chapter 3.)

The second method uses two VCRs. Use one VCR as a source deck and the second VCR as the record deck. Run a patch cord out of the "video out" and the "audio out" of the source deck and plug in the other ends into the "video in" and "audio in" of the record deck, paying close attention not to accidentally switch the two cords.

Make a short test once you've connected the camcorder to the VCR and play it back on another VCR that's connected to a TV. Make sure the record VCR's speed is SP, which stands for short play. LP and SLP, which stand for long play and super long play, respectively, are not acceptable tape speeds because the resolution will be too grainy. Standard VHS tapes can record over six hours in SLP speed because the tape runs three times

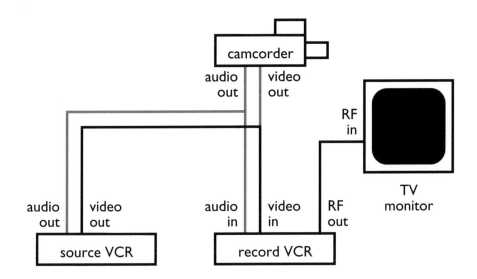

To duplicate a tape you need either a VCR or a camcorder as the playback source and a VCR as the recorder, or duplicator. A TV hooked up to the recording VCR will allow you to monitor the duplicating process.

slower than SP. VHS tapes in LP speed will last four hours, and SP speed lasts two hours. In general, the faster the speed, the better the resolution.

This is a long project, but one that will be rewarding if you have the time and energy to complete it. Who knows? Maybe your video yearbook will be so good your school or group will want someone to make one every year. You'll create a new tradition.

Music Videos

Music videos can be very exciting little films. They use images to reflect the character of a piece of music. They communicate styles and moods very effectively, and variety abounds. Watch some music videos, and you'll see everything from straight concert shots to elaborate, dramatic scenes in which the lyrics are acted out, to bizarre combinations of mysterious images.

Today's music videos cost hundreds of thousands of dollars and use professional video and sound equipment and personnel. Needless to say, your camcorder won't be able to produce such quality, so before you start buying sequin-studded clothes, custom guitars, and plane tickets to exotic locations, keep in mind that you will have to settle for a "refreshing raw quality" instead of the fancy effects achieved in Hollywood's million-dollar productions. You *can*, however, make a good music video. MTV might not want to air it, but it should look professional enough to impress your friends and family. And what it lacks in polish it can make up for in imaginative quality.

You can put yourself into a music video or you can film your musician friends. There are a couple of different methods you can use. First let's look at the method that's easiest to produce on an inexpensive camcorder.

Pick your music. It doesn't matter what you pick—an oldie, country and western, heavy metal, or rap. Just make sure you can visually portray the lyrics or the *mood* of the lyrics.

For example, if the lyrics of the song describe walking down to a river, you need to decide whether you need an actual river (and whether you have one nearby). If you live in a desert, the song "Take Me to the River" might not be right. On the other hand, the desert might be a clever counterpoint to the lyrics. You can crawl helpless and thirsty in a desert (which could be a small beach by your house as long as you're careful to frame it in such a way so as not to see the water) while the singer screams, "Take me to the river."

The easiest way to make a music video of your own performance with limited equipment is to turn on a stereo system and stand in front of the camera while acting and lip-synching to the music.

Find a room with the widest white wall that will serve as a backdrop for you to stand and dance in front of, and do something. You can dance, march, stand, stare—anything. You might find dancing is a good choice because it not only makes you move to the music, but it also is probably the most popular movement used by music-video stars.

Try to think of your own unique movement. You could combine running with the song "Running with the Wolves." You could mimic playing a trombone while you march to the song "76 Trombones." You could also do something less obvious. The important thing is to come up with ideas and images that you can actually capture on film.

Getting Your Equipment Together

We will be using three of the clip-on lights that we've used with standard lightbulbs in the previous chapter, but this time we will use two different-colored bulbs. You can use the red and green lightbulbs available at any hardware store. Don't use wattages that are too strong for your portable clip-on lights, or you'll start a fire. Place the colored lights near the floor at the base of the white wall and reflect them off the wall in an upward direction. The wall should appear flooded with red and green light through the frame of the viewfinder.

To properly light yourself as you stand in front of this beautifully colored wall, use the third clip-on light with a regular lightbulb. Direct this light toward the area where you'll be standing. You might want to reflect it off a white surface such as a nearby wall, a white posterboard, or the ceiling. Be careful not to wash out the red and green light on the wall.

Set up the camcorder on a tripod far enough from the wall so that you have some room to move. Dancing will necessitate a long shot that includes both the feet and the head, along with plenty of room to spare.

The biggest production challenge with this method of videomaking is getting the music to sound good on the tape. You could just blast the stereo inside the room where you're doing the videotaping, but you can do better.

Blasting the sound into the room will cause too much echo, and the music will be a big, muddy mess. Instead, try transferring your stereo signal directly to the camcorder with a patch cord. I suggest visiting a local Radio Shack or other electronics store and asking a salesperson for the best adaptors and patch cord to use. You will be hooking a patch cord directly from your stereo's output to the audio input of your camcorder.

If you don't want to bother with the patch cord setup, then you should try to get the stereo speakers as close as possible to the camcorder and its on-camera microphone.

When you've finally got all of this together, it's time to say, "Lights . . . camera, action!" Dance, sing (lip-synch) with the music, and move around a lot.

So what about all the quick edits to distant and exotic lands with all those costume changes that you see on MTV? Well let's examine exactly how those flashy videos are made. Then you'll understand why your equipment won't measure up.

How the Pros Make Music Videos

The first thing produced in most music videos is the musical soundtrack, which is usually part of the album production. In most cases, the music star concentrates on the music and has absolutely no idea what the music video will be like.

Once the music tracks are finished for a song and it's ready to be put on the compact disc, the music star's video producer will plan out each scene so that it goes along with the song. The song is then played on location at each video set. The different sets could range from a kitchen in New York to a ski jump in Switzerland.

Regardless of where the scene is, the video crew plays portions of the prerecorded CD on the video set so the music star can lip-synch the words. Although he or she sang the lyrics in the recording studio for the recording of the CD, the singer doesn't necessarily have to sing anything while they're videotaping him or her pretending to sing on the video set. When you see the finished music video on TV, it looks as though the music star is really singing in that kitchen or on the ski jump in Switzerland.

To make sure the music and the singer's lip movements in different sets stay in synch, special equipment coordinates the motors of the video cameras and the music playback units with an inaudible pulse signal that tells all the equipment how fast to run.

This synchronization of music and video is one of the factors that prevents you from making a professional music video. It is impossible to start and stop your audio playback precisely and move your video background to another location. Actually, it would be impossible to stop your audio playback at all, because once you start it up again there'll be a glitch or blank spot just long enough to disrupt the rhythm of the music.

Unfortunately, unless you have a spare $1 million to spend on the latest video and audio recording gear, or a spare $100,000 to pay video and audio producers to make a music video, you'll have to work with the equipment you have and your creativity.

If lip-synching isn't exactly what you had in mind, there's another method you can use to make a music video.

Because of karaoke technology, you can make a music video with your camcorder and actually sing on it. Karaoke, which is a Japanese word meaning "symphony without voices," is a hot trend in the United States.

For karaoke, popular music is recorded without the voices. Take Madonna's song "Vogue," for example. You can buy a karaoke version of the song on audiocassette. It will sound exactly like Madonna's music, but her voice will be missing. Your job, as a karaoke singer, is to provide the lead vocals on the tape.

There are tens of thousands of karaoke audiotapes available today. You might not find too many songs from unestablished groups like Jane's Addiction, Run DMC, or the Spin Doctors. But you'll find a big selection of popular Top-40 songs, like "Jump" by Van Halen, "Yesterday" by the

Jacks on camcorders accept accessories such as remote controls, external microphones, or headphones. On the upper left is the mini-plug jack for a wired remote control; the mini-plug jack on the upper right is a headphone jack; the three RCA jacks in the middle are for two audio outputs and one video output.

Beatles, or Elvis Presley's "Love Me Tender," which come in a variety of musical keys to fit anyone's vocal range.

You can find these karaoke audiotapes in a variety of stores. Try looking in the Yellow Pages under "Music Stores—Retail." This type of product is becoming so popular in the United States that now there are karaoke specialty stores called "singing shops." Your local mall might have a singing shop that stocks thousands of karaoke tapes.

Another way of conquering the same problem—getting prerecorded music without lead vocals—might be in your own collection of music. Think back and try to remember if any of your records, cassettes, or CDs have an instrumental (instruments only, no voices) version of a popular song. You can sing with the instrumental version of a popular song for your music video.

Once you've selected your music, you must solve a big production problem. How do you play back the music on your stereo and amplify your voice so it sounds like your voice is really part of the prerecorded song you're singing with?

There are several methods of dealing with this problem.

No External Microphone?

If you don't have a microphone, can't borrow one, and can't afford to buy your own, try this approach. It will take several tests to get the levels adjusted just right. Position the speakers of your stereo system close to the camcorder's on-camera microphone, but adjust the volume softer than you might normally play the music if you were lip-synching. Make sure the camcorder is within five feet of where you'll be singing. Be sure to project your voice loudly and clearly. Play back a test on your VCR and judge whether your voice can be heard slightly above the music. Make believe you've never heard the song before, and then judge whether you can identify all the words. Then go back and make an adjustment on your setup. You can't sing much louder, so you'll probably be turning the music up or down.

Using a Microphone Through the Stereo System

If you have a microphone, you'll have to determine where it can be plugged in. You might have a microphone input jack on your stereo system at home. This might allow you to plug the microphone into the stereo and sing along with the tape while amplifying it through the stereo system.

Using a Microphone Through the Camcorder

You might have two microphone inputs on your camcorder. You can plug the music (with a patch cord coming from your stereo system) into one microphone jack and plug your microphone into the other microphone jack.

There are many variations of these setups if you understand the fundamentals of video and audio recording. For example, with an audio tape deck that allows you to record two channels separately, you could record your voice on one channel and record the karaoke audiotape on the other channel. Then you could lip-synch during the actual videotaping of the music video. Not only would it look like you're singing live right on the music video, but it would actually be your voice mixed with the music.

Achieving Good Video Presence

Finally, you must think about video presence, either your own or that of the musicians you're filming. Video presence is similar to stage presence, which is how people handle themselves on a stage in front of an audience. I'm sure you've seen students acting on stage who seem small and uncomfortable. They may be turned away from the audience, speak too softly and in a monotone, or generally appear dull and lifeless. Such behavior indicates poor stage presence. But what about actors who project their voices so all can hear, look continually at the audience, and, in general, are comfortable and beaming with enthusiasm and energy? Those actors have good stage presence.

Likewise, a person with poor video presence moves very little, doesn't smile, doesn't pronounce words well, and talks in a monotone voice without inflection. There's a good word to describe successful video presence: *charisma.* A famous example of charisma is the difference between the images of 1960 presidential rivals John Kennedy and Richard Nixon. During the campaign Kennedy was perceived by most to have more charisma and appeared the more friendly and personable of the two, especially on television. Nixon's manner was more serious and business-like. Kennedy was relaxed; Nixon seemed stiff.

To achieve a strong video presence for yourself or those you're filming, follow these tips:

1. Always look directly at the camcorder lens. This doesn't mean holding your head in the same pose throughout the video, however. Using a mirror for practice, try turning your head to one direction while keeping your eyes looking forward. Or try moving your face downward with your eyes projecting upward at the camcorder. A smiling, enthusiastic facial expression might be the best face for you to put on, but then again, you've got to flow with the mood of the video. If you're singing a sad song, you might want a more sullen face.

2. Keep moving. Nothing looks worse than someone singing on a videotape while his or her shoes appear nailed to the floor.

Instead, move with the music. If you can't dance very well, at least rock back and forth or wiggle, or move your feet around. The more uncoordinated your feet are, however, the less of your lower body should be seen through the camcorder. Let's hope, though, that we'll see more than a close-up of your face.

3. Try making some arm and hand movements that describe the lyrics you're singing or lip-synching. At the word "you," point your finger at the camera. At the word "my," you can point to yourself. At the word "everything," you can put both hands facing upward and outward from your sides. So, at the line "You are my everything," you could point toward the lens, then point toward yourself, and then stretch both hands outward from your sides.

If the lyrics don't say something you can show with your hands, then move to the music by snapping your fingers or clapping your hands. Use the music to its fullest advantage. Remember, the music is really the star here. All the action on screen should complement the music. A strong music video is one that leaves the viewer wanting to hear more.

6

The Art of the Interview

Do you know where your grandparents were born? Do you how they met? Do you know what they did for fun when they were young?

A great way to develop your interviewing skills is to make a living documentary for future generations of your family to watch and enjoy. You can interview a grandparent, another older relative, or your own parents.

But before you interview your subject, let's go over a few interviewing and equipment principals.

The room used for interviewing should be well lit, very quiet, and have dry acoustics. Dry acoustics means there is very little echo. Rooms that are acoustically dry usually don't have wooden floors or other hard surfaces that sound can bounce off. Instead, they have soft, sound-absorbing furnishings such as draperies, rugs, beds, and sofas.

Next, make sure you use a tripod and position the camcorder close to the subject. A close camcorder, placed four to eight feet away, will pick up more of the subject's voice as opposed to the echo of the room. For this project you might want to borrow or rent a lavaliere microphone. Unlike the handheld microphone, the lavaliere is a tiny microphone, about the size of a peanut shell, that easily clips onto a lapel or shirt collar.

Because subjects don't hold it and really can't see it unless they make an effort to look straight down at their chests, they'll forget about it after a while. The microphone will just stay there on their collar giving you great sound. The lavaliere microphone is another example of the many types of external microphones available as substitutes for the on-camera microphone.

The lavaliere is such a good microphone for this type of video project that it doesn't matter if the room is dry (little echo) or live (lots of echo) acoustically. The close position of the lavaliere to the human voice doesn't allow much room for echo to get on videotape.

Keeping a Watchful Eye with Monitors

Next, you'll want to use a monitor for this project. A monitor is a small television (preferably color). The monitor will do several things for you.

First, you won't have to close one eye and look through the camcorder's tiny viewfinder every time you want to monitor the picture you're receiving.

Second, you can keep a watchful eye on the white balance (how colors appear) throughout the interview. You never know what could happen. An automatic light nobody knows how to shut off might cast a brownish color on your subject. Or moving the camcorder to a different position halfway through the interview might let a different type of light into the camcorder.

Third, monitors are great for fine-tuning the focus. Because they're very small, viewfinders aren't very good for focusing. But if you have a nine-inch, thirteen-inch, or larger monitor to look at, you can see exactly what the picture will look like when you play it back on a television after the interview.

Automatic focus is fine for some occasions, but not for this one. When it's zoomed in on a person's face, the camcorder takes a radar-like reading off the subject's face, somewhat similar to the method a bat uses to fly at night. If the camcorder reads the subject to be exactly four feet and six inches away, it automatically adjusts the lens to be in focus with this focal length. During the interview, if that person leans forward slightly—let's say to four feet and five inches away from the camcorder—the radar picks this up and adjusts the zoom lens accordingly. Since most people can't sit perfectly still for more than a few seconds, every time the subject

The white-balance function (WB) tells the camcorder what is white. Once the camcorder knows how colors appear under ambient light conditions, it can provide true color renderings.

moves, the camcorder adjusts. This makes a very jumpy picture that's not much different from the wobbly picture of a handheld camcorder.

Be sure to turn off the automatic focus, if possible. Your camcorder might have an auto/manual switch that covers all types of functions, such as automatic focus and white balance, or your camcorder might have an auto/manual switch solely for the automatic-focus function.

On older camcorder models, you can check if the automatic focus is turned off by running them in "standby" or "record" mode. Look at the lens. If it's moving back and forth automatically as you move it to different areas of the room, the automatic focus is still operating. If it's not moving back and forth, then it's in the manual position, and you will have to focus it when the distance between the subject and the camcorder changes.

Newer camcorder models focus electronically instead of mechanically. In other words, you should not see any moving parts. However, you might see images move in and out slightly, even with the most minute change in distance between the subject and the camcorder. If this happens, the camcorder is focusing too finely, when it should just keep the same focus. Constant focusing is too distracting for the viewer.

Hooking up a monitor to your camcorder is easy. There are several methods you can use. Read the instructions of your owner's manual and use the method that's best for your camcorder.

Once your monitor is hooked up, be sure to turn the sound down on the monitor while you're videotaping the interview or you'll get feedback. Also, check whether your camcorder is broadcasting its signal on channel 3 or 4. The monitor should be tuned to the same channel.

Since the monitor is showing you what you're recording but the sound is turned down, you'll need to hear the audio portion of the videotaping. You can hear the audio with a good set of headphones plugged into the headphone jack of the camcorder (usually labeled "ear" or "earphone"). If you don't have headphones, borrow your friend's Walkman or port-able cassette headphones. Hearing the audio is imperative if you're using an external microphone because something could go wrong with the hookup, or the cable could become disconnected halfway through pro-duction. If something went wrong with the audio, you would never know it until the interview was over and you reviewed the videotape.

Once you get your equipment set up and your subject in place, do a thirty-second test, and play it back on your monitor. Be sure to turn up the volume on your monitor when you are playing the test. Check the test for picture and sound quality.

Once you've finished your test, it's time to get your questions ready. Since this is an interview both for people who will and will not know your subject, be sure to clearly identify him or her. For example, your grandmother obviously knows your grandfather very well, but a distant relative or someone not born yet might not know your grandfather from a Martian. No question is too obvious for the interview.

Preparing Your Questions

Start with what might seem to be simple questions—the subject's name, age, and relationship to your family. Once you've established the answers to these questions, the following list of other questions will get you started.

1. Where were you born? When?
2. What's the earliest recollection you have of your childhood?
3. What were your parents' first and last names?
4. What were your parents' occupations?
5. Where were your parents born?
6. What was the name of your elementary school?
7. What was your favorite grade and teacher's name? Why?
8. How many brothers and sisters were there in your family, and what are their names and ages?
9. Where do your brothers and sisters live now, and what do they do?
10. What hobbies and activities did you have as a child?
11. What high school did you attend, and what was your fondest memory there?
12. What was your favorite high-school subject, and why?
13. What did you do after high school; that is, did you get a job or go to college?
14. Who was your first girlfriend or boyfriend?
15. When did you get married? Where did you meet your spouse?
16. How many children do you have?
17. What do the children do now for a living, and where do they live?

18. Where were you during World War II?
19. What were your thoughts during that period?
20. What was your opinion of U.S. participation in the Vietnam War?
21. Who are your heroes?
22. Name the occupations you've had and the companies you've worked for throughout your life.

These twenty-two questions are meant to get you started. You should be able to compose at least twenty-two more that are more personal. Ask questions about special events in your subject's life. Your mom or dad should be able to provide you with some good questions to ask your grandfather or grandmother.

The above questions will establish your interviewee's life and character, but to add more color, try asking some questions like:

1. What was your first kiss like?
2. What was the most embarrassing situation you've ever been in?
3. Describe your closest encounter with the police.

See if you can compose some questions that are even crazier. Remember, the serious questions make a good comprehensive interview, but unless you throw in a few zingers, your audience just might fall asleep. Try to ask open-ended questions that will draw out good storytelling.

Preparing Your Subject

Once your equipment and questions are ready, it's time to get the interviewee ready. You must prepare your subject. Be sure to tell him or her that the interview will take at least one hour. Don't worry, and don't start scrambling around looking for a few hundred more questions to fill the hour. You'll be surprised how much time it takes to answer twenty to thirty questions, especially if you're successful in getting your subject to elaborate.

Help your subject to relax and settle into a nice comfortable chair. Talk casually with him or her for a minute or two before starting the interview. This might be the best time to do your test. It might not be a good idea

Keep this in mind when you want to get an interesting shot of an individual: you might want to have shots of your interviewee walking through his or her home or neighborhood. If the subject is facing anywhere but straight at the camcorder, you must put more space in front of the subject's face than behind his or her head. This is called "leading" the subject. It is especially important when he or she is walking laterally in front of the camcorder.

to show the test to the subject, because nobody likes what they look like on videotape.

Tell your subject to look at the camera most of the time. You also might have to remind him or her several times during the interview to look at the camcorder lens. Most subjects will probably look at you because you'll be asking them the questions. They forget about the camera and just look at you as though they're in a conversation with you. Perhaps sit close to the camcorder so it will look as though the subject is looking at the lens although he or she is actually looking at you.

Remember that your subject is going to be very self-conscious about being videotaped. This is especially true of older people who haven't had a lot of experience with camcorders. Everyone is at least a little self-conscious about his or her looks. It's your job to make your subject comfortable in front of the camera. Look through the camera and tell your subject he or she looks good and is doing a nice job. Remind the subject to elaborate and say as much as possible about every question.

The final preparation before you begin is framing and checking for glare. You might want to start with the lens in a wide-angle position to establish the entire figure of the subject and the surroundings of the room. Then, halfway through the first few questions, slowly zoom in to a close-up of the subject's face. Leave it there for the rest of the interview. You won't have to look at the monitor continually, but be sure to look at it once in a while, especially if you notice the subject has moved during the interview.

After framing, check to see if there is any glare off the subject's glasses. Glare might come from the extra lights you've planted in the room, or reflective glare might come from windows behind you. You can eliminate the glare by closing the curtains around the windows, moving the light source, or moving your subject to a different position.

As a special added effect try the fade-in on your camcorder (if it has this feature). Camcorders can fade in from black to the image, or fade out from the image to blackness. In this instance you'll want to fade in. First center the subject with the lens in the desired position, then press the fade-out button. The screen on your monitor will become blank. Then, when you're ready to begin the interview, start the camcorder recording, wait ten seconds for the camcorder to get up to full speed, and press the fade-in button.

Video titles don't have to be fancy and produced by expensive character generators. Instead, add some creative touches by drawing titles for your video project.

If your camcorder has a titling feature, or if you have made your own titles by hand, then add the title during this ten-second blank period. A title could read "The Exciting Life and Times of Grandma Jones." Since you worked so hard putting the interview together, be sure to give yourself credit for the production. The credit should follow the title and could read "Interviewed and Videotaped by John Doe."

To add some visual variety, you might want to zoom back occasionally during the interview and show more of your subject, although the majority (about 70 to 80 percent) of your interview should be in the close-up position. We want to see the subject's face clearly when he or she changes expressions. If the camcorder is close enough, it can show joy in the face of the subject as he or she talks about his or her wedding or show tearful eyes as the subject recalls a death in the family. You can't anticipate emotions like these, so you had better be ready when the subject cries, laughs, or fondly recalls past events. The best way to be ready is to be zoomed in for a close-up.

After the interview, fade out to a blank screen. At the end of the film put the title "The End," along with a copyright, which tells what year the video was made and that parts of your interview can't be used for other things without your permission. A copyright title looks like this: "Copyright 1993 by Jane Doe."

Who knows? Your grandmother might become famous and NBC will need parts of your interview for the big documentary it is producing on her life.

It is most likely, however, that your video will be a personal and interesting video about someone who's very important to your family. And, in the process of making this keepsake, you'll learn how to draw people out on film—a skill that will come in handy during your future filmmaking career.

One last note: you can also be less formal and substitute the art of conversation for the structured interview. You might be inspired by the film *My Dinner with André*, which consists of two men talking over dinner. Filming a conversation enables you to reveal your subject's personality and ideas—as well as your own.

Commercials

When television was first seen, the commercials were pretty straight-forward. There were smiling car salesmen and singing detergent boxes. Most commercials were simple, cheerful sales pitches. Today, faced with an audience who has seen it all, the creative staffs at big advertising agencies have to keep coming up with new ideas, witty scenes, or stunning images to sell their clients' products. The TV commercial is becoming increasingly slick and even weird. Sometimes the product isn't even mentioned until the very end, or it is blatantly pushed on the viewer with a hard-edged script. Other commercials revert to the old style and use nostalgia to sell the product. Some products, such as Good and Plenty candy, have even started re-airing their vintage commercials. Putting together a commercial has become an exercise in cleverness.

You may not want to sell any products, but you, too, can make a television commercial just for the fun and challenge of it. Making a commercial will improve your powers of persuasion, something every beginning filmmaker needs to do. Since most commercials are either thirty or sixty seconds long, you don't have to spend a great deal of time actually filming. As a matter of fact, it will probably take more time to set up the production than to videotape it.

While your commercial doesn't have to be exactly thirty or sixty seconds long, that length is the TV industry standard. TV networks sell airtime (commercial time) during TV shows such as the Super Bowl in thirty- or sixty-second segments. A company like Pepsi will spend as much as $300,000 just for one thirty-second commercial! If the commercial is only twenty-nine seconds, Pepsi has wasted $10,000. If it's 31 seconds long, the TV network won't accept the commercial at all.

Your commercial, however, won't be aired during the Super Bowl or even a regular TV show, so don't worry about the length. Today there are also "infomercials," lengthy advertisements (lasting usually a half-hour or hour) for a single product, usually on cable stations or UHF channels early in the morning. Infomercials tend to be pretty boring, not creative or interesting, but you might like to try to make one as a satire.

Watch a wide variety of commercials, and spend some time thinking about their different approaches to the objective—selling the product. Figure out what style of commercial most intrigues you, and set out to make one along those lines. Obviously you won't have a big budget, but you can always compensate with creativity.

First you need a product to sell. It can be a real product or some phony product you make up yourself. It might be a soft drink, such as "Pop-e-Roni—the pop with a greasy pizza flavor," or a new kind of athletic shoe or no-frills airline.

Let's take a fictitious product: Pupper-Mints. Now think of a short slogan that tells the audience what's so great about it: "Pupper-Mints—when every bite counts." Or "Pupper-Mints—it brushes your dog's teeth while he eats."

Next you need to make a package of the product. You could spend weeks on this alone and create something really beautiful or strange, but if you want to come up with something fast, just take an empty cereal box and wrap white typing paper around it. It won't cover the box completely, but that's OK, because you won't be showing both sides of the box to the audience.

Once you've wrapped the paper tightly around the box, put creases on the corners, but don't tape it to the box just yet. Take the paper off the box and lay it flat on a table and draw your design. First you need the product name, *Pupper-Mints*, in big fancy letters. Next you need a big picture of

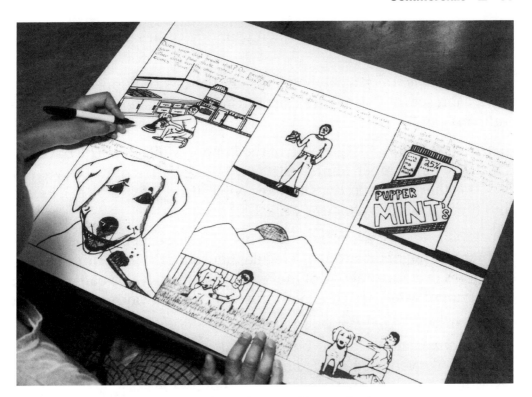

A storyboard helps you plan out and organize your video production.

a goofy-looking dog holding a Pupper-Mint and biting into it. At the bottom of the box comes the slogan, "When every bite counts," or "It brushes your dog's teeth while he eats," in normal lettering.

Once you've finished the box label in bright vibrant colors, put it back on the box and secure it with tape. Now it's time to plan your commercial.

Plan on a commercial that's thirty seconds long. Be careful not to write too long a commercial. You can always add material later if you need to.

Once you've decided on the length, draw a storyboard showing the action of the commercial. A storyboard is the plot of the story drawn in pictures. Try to limit your storyboard to approximately six pictures. (This will be a pretty basic, direct-sales commercial and, thus, a good first effort.)

Let's use our fictitious Pupper-Mints as an example.

Storyboard Picture #1: A kitchen. A boy empties a box of Pupper-Mints into a dog dish. He looks up at the camera and says, "Does your dog's breath stink? Do people give your dog a paw shake instead of a kiss? Do other dogs run the other way when your dog comes trotting down the street?"

Storyboard Picture #2: The boy holds up the box of Pupper-Mints and says: "You see 'ol Bonzo here can't brush his teeth after every meal like humans can."

Storyboard Picture #3: Close-up of the Pupper-Mints box. The boy says, "So I give him Pupper-Mints—the tasty breath mint that will leave your dog breathless. You see, dogs are like people. Food gives them bad breath but they can't brush after every meal."

Storyboard Picture #4: A large drawing of a dog's teeth. A toothbrush (which you might make out of a regular household broom) brushes back and forth over the drawing of the teeth while the boy (off-camera) says: "But Pupper-Mints act like a toothbrush and brush away remnants of last night's garbage-can raid."

Storyboard Picture #5: The boy bends down, pets the dog, and says, "Sounds like your dog needs Pupper-Mints." He bends his head down even further to hug the dog, smells the dog's breath, but frowns and quickly jumps up while holding his nose.

Storyboard Picture #6: Picture of boy petting the dog again while he says: "So when your dog has everybody running the other way . . . give him Pupper-Mints."

Now you're ready to videotape the commercial. First, decide what the best choice of location is. If your product is a food product, you might use the kitchen. If it's a bath product, try filming in the bathroom. If it's a soft drink or candy or new long-distance service, you'll probably want to film outdoors or in interesting indoor settings—probably with people who look like their lives are the most fun ever because they use the product.

The next consideration is lighting. What type of lighting is in your location? Is it natural light from a window, or is it artificial lighting? You might want to try a test before you begin your commercial. Just point the camera at the location, run and stand in the area you planned in your storyboard, and run a test of about twenty seconds.

Look at your test on a real TV, not just in the viewfinder. Does the picture have good resolution? Is the resolution as good as videotapes you've made outside in bright sunshine? Compare an outdoor videotape with the tape you just made indoors. Chances are you'll see more grain, but you may be able to improve the quality of the interior videotape by adding lights.

First make sure all the lights in the kitchen are on full power. Place a lamp or a torchère (a lamp that points up) high and behind the camera. Take more tests after you add more light, and you'll notice the grain disappear and the resolution improve.

Try complementing the natural light that is coming in through the window. For example, if the natural light illuminates the left side of a subject's face, place the artificial light on the darker, right side to balance it.

If your kitchen has a window, try positioning your camcorder so the window is behind it or to the side of it. Don't point the camcorder directly at a window or your subject will be backlit.

Next make sure the camcorder is as close as possible to the subject so that the on-camera microphone will pick up the subject's voice without much echo. Also make sure there is no interfering noise, such as neighborhood lawn mowers, babies crying, hammering, or whatever noise might ruin your soundtrack.

Now think back to the Pupper-Mints commercial. The last scene, which the viewer sees but which isn't included on the storyboard, should be a close-up of the Pupper-Mints box with a short musical jingle in the background.

A jingle is the music that accompanies a commercial. You might hear the jingle throughout the commercial, like in many soft-drink or fast-food commercials, or you might hear it only in the last five or ten seconds of the commercial (the latter is called a "tag"). Advertisers use jingles because they subconsciously persuade the viewer to buy the product. How many times have you caught yourself humming or singing the jingle of a TV commercial? Believe it or not, the more you sing about a product, the more likely you are to buy it when you see it on the store shelf.

Let's say our jingle tag at the end of the Pupper-Mints commercial is going to be ten seconds long. Here's what we'll sing: "Pupper-Mints . . . Pupper-Mints . . . they'll leave your dog breathless." Now try to fit those words to a melody. Once you've made up a catchy little song either accompany yourself on a keyboard, guitar, or other musical instrument or a friend to play an instrument for you. Combine the instrumental music with the melody you've composed and you're ready to put the jingle tag at the end of your commercial.

To insert the last scene of the Pupper-Mints commercial, cue up the videotape at the first blank spot after storyboard scene #6, put the camcorder on record/pause, and fill up the entire frame with the box of Pupper-Mints. When you, your musicians, and extra singers (if any) are ready, gather around the microphone of the camcorder, release the record/pause button, and record the close-up of the Pupper-Mints box and the jingle.

Whatever product you come up with, make sure you prompt the viewer to react, whether you make a plea to buy, use, or give something. Provoke a response.

Comedy

Comedy is a great way to reach an audience. Whether you prefer the physical comedy of the Three Stooges or the verbal wit of Woody Allen, you can be certain that others share your sense of humor. As a filmmaker, you can delve into your own ideas about what's funny and what isn't and then experiment with ways to share those ideas with others. Making a comedy movie is not only great fun; it is also quite gratifying: making people laugh is a great achievement.

There are many different formats you can use to make a comedy. You can simply turn on the camera, stand in front of it, and do your own stand-up routine. Or you can do your own slapstick comedy, running into the wall or getting squirted with the garden hose. You can be the star, or you can write a comedy script and find good funny actors to perform it. If you're like most aspiring videographers, you'll probably want to stay behind the camera.

You need to start by asking yourself what's funny. You probably won't know for sure until you put some scenes on videotape. Play them back for an audience, and monitor the response you get. Of course your friends and relatives will be more gentle to your work and forgive even the dumbest things you try to portray as comedy. If you want a more honest opinion, I recommend playing your comedy to an impartial crowd that doesn't owe you a laugh.

One of my students came up with a very simple production that received a great many laughs when she showed it to an audience. All it took was a camcorder, a baby in a crib, a baby blanket, and a Harry Connick, Jr., song on CD.

Her idea was to make it seem like the baby was singing the song "New York, New York." How did the baby do it? Just a little trick photography, that is, videography. With a camcorder on a tripod focused on a headshot of the baby, the videographer hid her hand under the baby blanket. While the song was playing into the microphone of the camcorder, she positioned the blanket up to the baby's chin to hide her finger, which pulled down the baby's bottom lip in time with the lyrics of the music. Ultimately it did look like the baby was singing the song. Who knows how long she had to rehearse to make the baby's mouth move on each syllable, but it resulted in a very funny and appealing comedy.

You can do something similar with another actor that won't let you down—the family pet. You can make a great comedy with your pet, who'll probably do anything you ask (without complaints). Although some people don't think animals are funny and using them *can* get a little tiresome, it can work well. In comedy we often find combinations of people (or animals) with unlikely expressions or abilities: your dog is talking, or a baby is singing. Another example could be a seemingly timid, elderly woman riding a Harley Davidson motorcycle. You might not be able to film a moving motorcycle but you can think of plenty of examples that you can film. The possibilities are endless.

Ruff the dog, Bob the cat, Polly the parrot, or even Thumper the rabbit all make great actors (in that order). I said, "in that order," for a reason. Dogs make great actors, and the smarter the dog, the better your video will be. Cats have the smarts for acting, but they're often too fickle and independent. If you're a cat lover, you'll soon be a cat hater once you try to videotape one.

Other pets like snakes, hamsters, rabbits, parrots, ferrets, or any other animal people try to keep in cages can be even harder to work with. You may be thinking about how smart the neighbor's parrot is because it says, "Rrraaarrrk, hello beautiful," whenever you walk through the doorway. Just remember, parrots don't know what they're saying, they merely imitate what people train them to say. And as for rabbits, snakes, and the rest . . . forget it. You'd probably get more of a video response from your pet rock.

One of my students used a dog for a comedy and actually made him talk, or *appear* to talk.

This project had two parts. First the videographer captured the dog as the main subject on videotape. Then with a stroke of genius (or the memory of the dog movie *Benji,* which used the same technique), he videotaped scenes from a dog's perspective by holding the camera about eighteen inches off the ground—about the height of a dog's head. In other words, the videographer made it appear as though the dog was talking, then showed what the dog was talking about from his own perspective.

First, leave twenty seconds of blank tape at the beginning, so you can add titles later (or go ahead and put them on tape).

To make it appear as though the dog was talking, the videographer placed peanut butter on the dog's tongue. If you have ever put peanut butter on a dog's tongue, you know what I'm talking about. Because of the stickiness of the peanut butter, the dog went into wacky gyrations trying to clear his pallet.

(*Obviously, you should not do anything cruel here. Make sure your dog likes peanut butter and use only a small amount.*)

As the student played back the tape, he perfectly timed his own words to coincide with the dog's mouth movements. In other words, he inserted or dubbed his own voice onto the video soundtrack. What made this videotape extra funny was the big booming voice the videographer used for the big husky dog. A high-pitched, squeaky voice might have fit a perfectly groomed poodle, if that had been the breed used.

To dub in an audio track that will make the animal appear to be talking, you'll need a special feature on your camcorder called "audio dub." When you audio dub the vocal track on your camcorder, you're in the record mode, but it doesn't record video. It's a good thing it doesn't record the video or else you would erase the existing video track that you're trying to dub over.

To audio dub you need a camcorder with an audio dub feature, but don't worry, there is a good chance your camcorder or a friend's camcorder has this function, because it's very common. You might need an external microphone, because some earlier camcorder models require a microphone other than the one on the camcorder itself.

Using a bath towel for a sling, a camcorder can be suspended two feet off the ground, giving the dog's perspective.

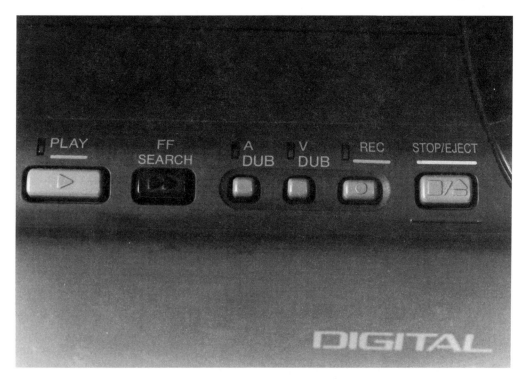

If you're lucky enough to have a video and/or an audio dub function on your camcorder, you can add a video track or audio track without erasing your existing material. For example, with an audio dub function, you can record over an existing audio track without erasing the accompanying video track. With a video dub, you can record over an existing video track without erasing the accompanying audio track.

Perform a quick test to find out if you can successfully dub an audio track without erasing the video track (don't use your project tape to test the audio, as you might accidentally erase it).

Once you've tried dubbing, it's time to try another technique my student videographer used: the "dog's-eye" view.

You can film in such a way so that the audience will seem to be viewing exactly what a dog is seeing—but get ready to wear out your knees. Put on some old pants, because you're going to be crawling with a camcorder. Since a dog's eyes are only about one or two feet off the ground, and you are trying to create the same perspective the dog sees, you need to be down there, too. This is not a new technique. If you haven't seen the movie *Benji*, it might be helpful to rent it. A low camera angle is used almost exclusively throughout the movie to give the dog's perspective.

The opposite would hold true for a video shot from a giraffe's perspective. You would have to film everything from a ladder and point the camera downward to give a perspective of what a giraffe sees every day.

To create the dog's perspective but avoid crawling in the mud, my student cradled the camcorder in a makeshift harness. The videographer held a bath towel at both ends and let the middle drop down in the form of a long skinny "U" shape. This enabled him to walk erect and still accomplish the dog's perspective.

The first shot of the video was an establishing shot depicting the dog coming out of the house and trotting to a stop on the front lawn. Next he shifted to the dog's perspective. Holding the camcorder in his harness approximately one foot above the ground, he created an establishing shot from the dog's perspective by panning the entire neighborhood, just as though the dog was inspecting the surrounding environment. Aways make slow, smooth flowing pan movements with the camcorder and avoid sudden, jumpy movements.

Next the videographer began shooting visuals for the rest of the outdoor portion of the script.

Since the videographer had a script to work from, it was easy to imagine which video scenes would look good with the words. Before you shoot anything for your project, write a detailed script—it can save you a lot of time later.

Once the videotape footage was finished, the videographer put the crazy dog voice on the soundtrack. Remember, the voice he put on the soundtrack was supposed to be the dog talking to himself.

After finishing all the shooting and the soundtrack, titles finished off the beginning of the videotape (twenty seconds of which was purposely left blank for the titles).

That's just how one comedy video unfolded using an animal actor. Your video might use human beings or aliens or talking vegetables.

Write Your Own Comedy Script

If you are serious about comedy, I suggest you try your hand at writing and filming a truly funny script. You will need to come up with a comic situation *and* funny dialogue. Then you will have to choose your actors wisely *and* be able to communicate well with them throughout the filming. Frankly, you will need every bit of creativity you have. Comedy is actually hard work, but when you progress from a funny script to a funny video you will experience the great pleasure of making people laugh.

I suggest you begin by thinking about funny situations you have experienced or witnessed. Do you want to film one person performing a constant stream of gags to a loose storyline or set up a more complex story that builds to a hilarious climax? Do you want to poke fun at prejudice? Do you want to show the funny side of a serious situation? Do you want a script that allows for a lot of physical comedy or would you rather come up with sharp, witty lines? Do you already have actors in mind? How might you showcase their comic abilities?

Try your hand at creating a funny situation and writing some dialogue. Read it aloud or ask your actors to read it for you. Think about comic timing as you watch your written lines turn into spoken dialogue. After you've rehearsed your script, ask yourself whether any lines can come out. You might be able to use visuals in place of dull, explanatory lines. Write a script that you can film fairly simply. Don't give yourself the extra burden of hard-to-film locations, expensive sets, or complicated special effects. It will be challenge enough to write a script that works. Most important, though, have fun being funny. And for more intensive advice about screenwriting, see chapter 9, which discusses the dramatic script.

I also recommend that you watch some classic funny films. Some are listed in chapter 13 of this book. Take a look at every kind of comedy, from film versions of Shakespeare's plays to classic Marx Brothers movies. Good comedies have certain similarities. Groucho and William weren't as different as you might think. Both were masters at coming up with clever comebacks, opportunities for slapstick, and very, very funny situations.

Following is an example of a simple comedy script. It shows the importance of thinking about the comic situation, the dialogue, *and* what you are going to do with the camera. Remember, the camera has the potential to be one of your comic elements. Use it to enhance the comedy. Camera instructions are an integral part of your script.

The Date
A Script by Pearl Frantz

It's Saturday night, and a teenage girl is nervously getting ready for a first date with a guy she's been hoping for weeks would ask her out. The first scene is in front of the bathroom mirror as she blow-dries her hair.

KRISTY: (*Talks loudly above the drone of the hair dryer*) My hair will look good, but I don't know what to wear tonight. Actually, I don't have anything to choose from. This night is going to be a disaster!

Cut to Michael's bathroom; he's blow-drying his hair.

MICHAEL: (*Talks loudly above the drone of the hair dryer*) Hmmm, I wonder what I should wear tonight?

Cut to Kristy's bathroom; she's standing in front of the mirror, wearing eyeglasses, knee socks, brown loafers, a plaid skirt, a white blouse, and orange suspenders.

KRISTY: (*Frowns*) Oh great, I look like Gertrude, the biggest nerd in school. Wait a minute, what if he picks me up on a motorcycle?

Cut to Kristy in the same position with different clothing. She's wearing a black leather jacket, black leather pants, spiked hair, and very heavy makeup.

KRISTY: VROOOOOOM! (*Forms her hands as if gripping handlebars of a motorcycle and talks into the mirror*) Hey Michael, want to pop some wheelies on your hog?

Cut to Michael in front of mirror beginning to tie a necktie around his neck.

MICHAEL: This ought to look good enough for Kristy. After all, she's a very sweet and innocent girl. It's a good thing I don't have a motorcycle; she'd probably never set foot on it.

Cut to Kristy wearing another outfit. It's a floral dress, white tights, white headband, and patent leather shoes.

KRISTY: I don't know what I could have been thinking. There's no way a guy like Michael—prom king, football quarterback, God's gift to women—is going to drive up on a motorcycle. He'll probably drive up in his dad's Mercedes. (*Looks at herself and frowns*) There's no way I'm leaving this house dressed like this. (*She turns sideways to look at her profile and sticks her tongue out*)

Cut to Michael who has traded his necktie for blue jeans and a red T-shirt with "Chicago Bulls" on it. Exterior camera shot of Michael walking up to Kristy's front door.

MICHAEL: (*As he knocks on the door*) Kristy is going to think I'm some kind of slob for wearing clothes like this, but I couldn't think of anything else. I guess the worst she could do is slam the door in my face.

Cut to Kristy, who is peering through the eye hole on the other side of the door and getting ready to answer the knocking. Camera angle does not reveal what she's wearing.

Cut to outside the door; the camera shows only Kristy's head as she opens the door.

KRISTY: (*In complete shock*) Oh no! (*Quickly slams the door in Michael's face*)

MICHAEL: I knew it. She probably thinks this outfit is really stupid.

Cut to interior. Kristy is standing with her back against the door she just slammed shut. Camera pulls back to show she's wearing an identical red, Chicago Bulls T-shirt with blue jeans.

KRISTY: (*Whimpers*) This can't be happening to me. I'm wearing the same thing he is.

Fade out

9

Writing and Videotaping a Script

In this chapter you are going to switch from comedy to drama and write a script and act it out to make a dramatic video. You will be the film director—the person who guides the actors and decides where to place the camera to capture the right mood—and the screenwriter. You might also choose to be an actor in the video.

The script is an important part of any video project that has dialogue. A script can make or break a movie. If the script is rotten, it doesn't matter how many cars they smash up or gags they pull—the movie won't be as good as it could have been.

What makes a good script? It would take a book larger than this to cover the basics of script writing. In fact, the number of books that already have been written on the subject of script writing could easily fill a bookstore.

Like playing an instrument or shooting a basketball well, good script writing takes years of practice. You don't have years to perfect your script writing right now, but if you follow a few basic principles, you can begin to hone your talent, and you will come up with something clever and interesting for your video.

One of the basic principals of a good script, whether it's for a feature film or a five-minute short subject, is conflict. When you write your script, no matter how long it is, make sure there's some type of conflict. Nearly every TV show or movie you've ever seen has conflict, since this is what draws the audience's interest.

What do I mean by conflict? Every day we experience it. Getting to school late is conflict. Failing a math test is conflict. Disappointing a friend or oneself is conflict.

Think of some of your favorite movies, and try to recall the conflict. There are few movies that don't have some problem for the main actors to resolve. The conflict in *Back to the Future* was Marty McFly's attempt to get back to 1985. In *Batman*, the main character's quest to eliminate the Joker is the movie's conflict and underlying theme.

Even TV shows have conflict. Just watch a soap opera and you'll see a handful of conflicts all in one show. Everybody has conflict, whether it's a girlfriend running away with a rock musician or Uncle Joe having an accident that leaves him paralyzed.

To get started on your script, think of a conflict with which you're familiar. It might be failing a test, or not getting a part in a play, or someone becoming angry with your political views. Build your script around the conflict.

Here's a script by my student G. K. Darby. There's no slapstick, no smashing cars, no outrageously wild visuals. This short video is all dialogue, creatively written, around a central idea, or conflict.

Camera is placed in the refrigerator.
Characters open refrigerator door and begin talking.

RITA: (*Starts digging around*) So I walk out on the porch and there's this partridge in a pear tree.

GEORGE: (*From behind her*) How unusual!

RITA: Yeah, it was pretty cute. (*Door closes*)

RITA: (*Door opens; she starts rummaging for milk*) The next day I find two turtle doves hopping around on the porch.

GEORGE: Joy. (*Door closes*)

GEORGE: (*Door opens*) So did the neighbors complain about the calling birds?

RITA: (*Slightly amazed George knew what happened next*) Yeah, and the French hens' hormones were totally out of control. It was unbelievable. I've never seen birds move that fast. They were all over . . . (*Door closes*)

RITA: (*Door opens*). . . So I forgave him for all the birds. I mean really! Five golden rings. One for each finger.

GEORGE: Sounds really romantic . . . Could you get an orange for me? Thanks. (*Door closes*)

GEORGE: Where did you meet this guy? Is he some sort of psycho?

RITA: I met him at an art gallery. He said he was into Super Modernism.

GEORGE: Those fresh eggs must have been nice.

RITA: Nice but a little messy. They laid them in the oddest places. I kept stepping on . . . (*Door closes*)

RITA: (*Door opens*) . . . I had to let the swans swim in the bathtub. The neighbors let me use their shower. I was so embarrassed.

GEORGE: Ahhh . . . very interesting . . . (*Door closes*)

GEORGE: (*Door opens*) So the police came?

RITA: And the Florida Department of Agriculture, the Humane Society, the riot squad, the . . . (*Door closes*)

RITA: (*Door opens; in a miserable tone*) It was a mess. The Lords a Leaping trampled the Pipers Piping, and the Drummers Drumming kept chasing after the Maids a Milking. The poor cows, oh those poor cows. They had nowhere to go. Feathers and cow dung filled the house.

GEORGE: Wow, what a guy. (*Door closes*)

GEORGE: (*Door opens*) . . . So you sued the bastard?

RITA: Yeah, I got my house back and now he's in the poor house! Could you hand me the milk?

GEORGE: Sure. (*Door closes*)

This script, although it's quite unusual, is simply good dialogue. Slowly the disruption of life that creeps in becomes the ensuing conflict in the script. You probably found yourself reading a little hastier as it went on to determine what would happen next.

The opening and closing of the refrigerator door separates the dialogue nicely, similar to the way fade in and fade out work.

The logistics of producing this videotape were easy. The director just put the camcorder in the refrigerator and let it run. Meanwhile, on the outside, the two main characters used good timing to give the viewer the idea of time passing during the blackouts (the door closing).

Once you have your script, you're ready to put it on videotape. You should also have planned out all the action that accompanies the dialogue.

In this book's appendix is another script written by some of my students. The content probably won't dazzle you, since it was written for a particular school activity, but I've included it so that you can familiarize yourself with the conventions of composing a videoscript. A script must be written with both dialogue and film directions included. I suggest you practice writing scripts that will truly work in terms of their spoken dialogue, their instructions for the person operating the camera, and the way the two are integrated.

Many scripts involve two characters walking and talking together. There are two ways to approach videotaping people walking. In one method you stand far from the subjects in a still position. While the characters walk toward the stationery camera, a slow zoom out manually captures the subjects as they come closer. In the other method you position the camera very close to the subjects. As the subjects walk forward, the camera itself moves backward at the same pace as the characters.

The second method is best because the camera as well as the on-camera microphone are close to the actors. Remember, the closer the microphone is to the subject, the better the sound will be. Good audio will make your video appear more professional. However, there is one drawback to the second method. As you take each step backward, you will tend to bounce or jerk the camera a little.

You can solve this problem by putting your camcorder on wheels. I know you don't have a $100,000 camera dolly in your garage, but you can make your own camera dolly out of odds and ends. Your old red wagon might make a good dolly as long as the wheels aren't rusty (you don't want squeaking sounds on the soundtrack). Just sit in the wagon, hold the camcorder securely, and have a friend pull you backward at the same speed of the subjects.

Another makeshift dolly is a wheelchair. Sit in the wheelchair and have an assistant move you backward as you videotape the characters. A wheelbarrow, too, would make a good dolly.

You can videotape the entire dialogue of your own script in one take as long as the two characters don't make any mistakes. That means your characters will need to rehearse and, most certainly, to memorize the script. This may take some time, and your friends who agreed happily to act in your video at first might start hating you when they see there's a lot of work involved. Don't worry, however, and try to be a firm disciplinarian and direct them to perfection. Once they see the finished product, they probably will want to act again in one of your video productions.

The above script was very short and simple. If you want your script to follow the formula professionals use, then try the "beginning, middle, and end" formula. These three sections are similar to acts in a play. Actually, most movies and TV shows use this three-part formula.

The beginning act is the time to introduce the main character—the hero—and the conflict he or she will be encountering throughout the production. If it's a second character or villain who creates the conflict, this is also the time to introduce him or her to the audience.

The middle act is where the conflict increases. Make it look to the audience as though absolutely nothing can save the hero. Never, ever, let the audience look far enough ahead to see the solution to the main character's problems.

In the third act the main character gets deeper into trouble and then somehow resolves the problem to end the story.

George M. Cohan, the famous composer of musicals who wrote songs such as "I'm a Yankee Doodle Dandy," "Over There," and "Give My Regards to Broadway," also wrote stories and plots for his musicals. He had a simple description of the three-act script. I will paraphrase it for you.

In the first act get your man (main character) up a tree (conflict). In the second act throw stones at him to the point he almost falls out of the tree. In other words, the conflict becomes so intense, he nearly perishes. Get the main character out of the tree in the third act (resolve the crisis or conflict).

Pretty simple, eh? About 99 percent of the stories you see on TV or in movies are developed around this formula.

Let's dissect this three-act format in the movie *Back to the Future*. The main character, Marty McFly, ends up in 1955 because of Dr. Brown's time machine. That's the conflict. But there are some smaller conflicts going on at the same time. Will Dr. Brown be dead from the terrorists' bullets if Marty ever gets back to 1985? Will Marty be able to drive his girlfriend to the camping trip they had planned for the weekend? We're also introduced to the villain, Biff, in the first act.

In the second act, Marty continues to get stones thrown at him. That is, a new conflict takes precedence over the other ones. Will he be able to get his parents to go to the high-school dance where they originally fall in love? If he doesn't, the other conflicts (Dr. Brown's death, his weekend camping trip, etc.) don't amount to much because Marty will never be born if his parents don't meet and fall in love with each other. Biff also helps to throw a few more rocks at Marty in his tree, if you recall.

The third act is the night of the dance, and still more complications arise. Will lightning strike the clock tower? Will Dr. Brown manage to channel the lightning's power to the time machine?

Of course, all comes out well as the third act winds down. All of the smaller conflicts are resolved. Dr. Brown survives because of a bullet-proof vest. Marty gets a new four-wheel-drive truck to go camping with because his parents are now successful and prosperous. Meanwhile, Biff turns into a buffoon.

There it is: the three acts of a script. And when you first saw *Back to the Future* you didn't even know this secret formula was unfolding. If you want to make a longer and more suspenseful script that will hold your audience's attention, make sure you follow the formula. The next time you watch a movie or your favorite TV show, look for the three-act formula. The idea is to use it without the audience knowing you've done so.

The Documentary

For some filmmakers, reality is more intriguing—and personally challenging—than fiction. Film, whether for the big screen or the home television, is a powerful communicator, and much of its history has been dedicated to exposing true stories and situations. Your documentary subject can be anything that explains or gives the viewer some knowledge on a subject. "Baby's First Steps," "Sister's First Date," "Dad's Broken Leg," etc., are simplistic examples, but your documentary could have great social value and serious impact.

Choosing Your Subject

Look around your neighborhood and city, and determine if there's a social injustice your audience needs to know about. Keep in mind that the documentary is often a way to expose a problem or controversy. Documentaries are thorough, often taking a subject (or a person) and explaining it (or him or her) in depth.

What about environmental pollution as a subject? Is a nearby abandoned factory leaking toxic waste or other destructive materials into the water supply? You won't have much problem finding environmental pollution. A river, lake, or even a garbage-littered street could be the focus of a documentary. Overcrowding at your school could be another issue. The many social problems our communities face should be obvious and easy to find no matter where you live.

Of course a documentary doesn't have to have social impact. Lighter topics could include the assembly of a science project, a biography of a person you find particularly interesting, or any other exposé of a person, place, or event.

You may think you've never seen a documentary, but your public broadcasting station (PBS) airs them regularly. Weekly PBS shows such as *The American Experience* or *Nova* document some type of subject for their audiences. News shows like *60 Minutes*, *20/20*, and *Primetime Live* are all shows that feature several fifteen-minute documentaries in every imaginable category. If you want to see one of the first great examples of the documentary, go to your library or video store and ask for a copy of "Harvest of Shame," Edward R. Morrow's famous CBS news report on the plight of migrant workers in the United States in the early sixties.

Some feature-length documentary films have become so successful they've been distributed nationally and shown at movie theaters. In the 1970s, *Woodstock*, the documentary on the legendary three-day rock-music festival, was highly successful. Another 1970s rock festival documentary, *Gimme Shelter*, began as just a concert film, but the director smartly refocused the film around an unexpected murder in the front rows. In the 1980s, *Roger and Me* was another famous documentary with enough mass appeal to make it to national distribution. It exposed the deterioration of the town Flint, Michigan, after General Motors closed its automobile plant there. These and other documentaries are available at libraries and video rental stores.

So just what subject should you choose, and how should you construct your own documentary? Don't try to produce feature-film length right off the bat. A ten-minute video will keep you busy for a number of days, and it will give you enough experience to get you started in documentary film production.

Pick a subject you'd like to make a comment on. Your documentary should ask a question and then answer it. For example, the subject of homeless people is quite broad. Your question could be this: "Can abandoned buildings in the city be renovated and transformed into housing for the homeless?" The film should pose this question to the viewer, and then answer it.

Your subject or question may encompass literally dozens of issues, but you should narrow it down to one, specific question. Picking too broad a subject makes it difficult to stay within the ten-minute time constraint. For example, a specific question that addresses one segment of the complex homeless issue is "Should the homeless be fed by money from the government or strictly by charitable donations?"

Besides asking and answering a question, the documentary should present the issue and some background. If indeed your subject is the homeless, you could give some history of the issue through newspaper and magazine clippings (found at the library) or with posters and photographs. You should also include interviews with people who have something interesting to say on the subject. Everybody has an opinion; your job is to get them to say it on videotape.

Point of View

Another important decision to be made is point of view. Do you want your documentary to be a nonbiased exposé of an issue that will give audience members enough information from opposing viewpoints to allow them to make their own judgments?

As the director of the film, you have the power to present any viewpoint you wish. If you think the plight of the homeless is not a problem at all, but more a product of too much media coverage, then present that viewpoint to the audience. It's your videotape, so you can do what you want.

Remember, as the filmmaker you are assuming some social responsibility with the view you take. Younger, more impressionable viewers might very well believe whatever you put on videotape, regardless of whether it's the truth or simply one view of the truth. Take care to be clear about the difference between the facts and opinions or interpretations of them. If you do present a definite view, be sure to get others to say it. It's more powerful if you interview someone on the street who says what you're trying to get across to the viewer. Obviously, if you're trying to portray the plight of the homeless simply as a media bonanza with no substance, you won't want to include an interview with someone who says the homeless situation is a real problem.

When you interview people for your documentary, don't include your voice asking the question during the interviews. It's not needed, and it subjects the viewers to more wordage than they need.

An outline of such a documentary might include these scenes:

1. A collage of different homeless people sitting on the street, begging, or sleeping in the park.
2. Newspaper clippings on homelessness.
3. Interviews with people on the street who have an opinion on homelessness.

What if you want to make something more hard-hitting? What would be the sequence of scenes then? Many times a documentary director tries to confuse the audience by presenting the opposite viewpoint first, then countering it throughout the film with the other side of the issue. By the time the end of the film rolls around, the audience has seen both sides of the issue, but decidedly has been led to believe the opposite of what the film presented at the outset.

With that strategy in mind, here is how you might present the viewpoint that the homeless situation is real:

1. Man on the street saying that homelessness is not a serious problem in this country but really a bunch of baloney exaggerated by the media.
2. Background on the scope of homelessness using newspaper clippings, posters, and actual homeless people on the street.
3. Interviews with several people who have the viewpoint that the homeless are in desperate need.
4. Interviews with actual homeless people explaining the problem of homelessness from personal experience.

When the audience hears the first person's viewpoint, it subconsciously tells them that this documentary takes the viewpoint that homelessness is not a real problem. But as the video continues, every segment thereafter presents the opposite viewpoint. By the time the ending title rolls around, you should have turned the audience 180 degrees and convinced them of the seriousness of the problem of homelessness.

Making Your Documentary

If you use interviews with people on the street, you most definitely will need to use an external microphone. You can use any microphone so long as it has at least six feet of cord to allow you to step back from the interviewee and still have good audio fidelity. Because you (or a helper, called a "gaffer" by Hollywood moviemakers) are holding the microphone close to the interviewee's mouth, unwanted street noise, such as passing cars and people talking nearby, will be minimized.

Once you're conducting your interviews, don't let any interviewee get away with just a yes or no answer. Keep probing by asking the same question differently until you get a satisfactory answer. One trick to getting a complete answer is to ask a question in such a way that the interviewee is forced to elaborate. Instead of asking "Do you think that homelessness is a serious problem in this country?" which could easily evoke a yes or no answer, ask the same question in this way, "How do you feel about the plight of homeless people in our city?" There's no way anyone can say just yes or no to that question.

If you want to drive your point of view home, pictures of homeless people in helpless situations, such as unsanitary sleeping conditions or a collage of distressed faces, will definitely affect your audience. It's always best to show it rather than say it. In this instance, pictures are certainly worth a thousand words, and they will make a bigger impact than anything you tell the audience through interviews or narration.

As an alternative to interviews, you could simply compile scene after scene, dubbing in narration to get the point across.

One pitfall you might encounter when making your documentary is lack of organization. To remedy this problem make an outline of your scenes. If you can't edit your videotape and you have to assemble the scenes inside the camcorder, it is especially important to plan your presentation in advance.

Keep your documentary in chronological order. For example, let's say your documentary is a day in the life of one homeless man, which, incidentally, is a pretty good topic. Your outline might look like this:

1. Waking up in the morning.
2. Cleaning up and wrapping up bedclothes.
3. Looking for food.

4. Eating breakfast.
5. Begging for money.
6. And so forth.

Obviously, falling out of chronological order, such as starting with breakfast and then following that segment with waking up, will confuse the audience.

Once you've compiled your scenes chronologically, make an interview tape and have that person describe his day.

You can add the audio portion two different ways. If your camcorder has an audio dub function, just slip it onto the original videotape where the person's viewpoints describe what's seen on the videotape. A different method is to add the audio while you're dubbing the master video onto a VCR deck. This method requires great organization of your audio tracks, so that you can add them at the right time, and so that they end up the same length as your video scene.

For example, during the interview the homeless man says, "I sleep in the alley by Kay's hardware store. It's pretty quiet there, but it does get pretty cold at times." That dialogue should not be longer than your segment showing the homeless man sleeping in the alley. In this instance, the homeless man is functioning as a narrator for his own video.

One final thing to remember is that whatever issue you choose, be sure to get proper permission to film people or their property.

I like the following script because it shows that the visuals are going to be used to their best advantage. The words and music have been carefully and thoughtfully joined to the images. The result is a moving, informative, and best of all, thought-provoking documentary.

Interracial Adoption
A Script for a Video Documentary by Christine Blomgren

Video	**Audio**

I. INTRODUCTION

Snapshots of children waiting to be adopted.	**Music:** Michael Jackson's "Heal the World."

Shots of the same children playing.

Narration:
"Today there are X number of children in the United States who are waiting to be adopted. The chance of them finding a family within the next year is minimal, and the older the children get, the risk of never being adopted increases.

"More than half of the children needing adoptive parents represent minority groups, and the numbers of minority families seeking children don't match the overwhelming number of children needing homes.

"Therefore, interracial adoption seems to be the only solution left to save these children. But, unfortunately, our society is not color blind, and racial segregation has been a major obstacle in the desperate search for parents for America's children."

Shot of graph showing statistics. See 1, 2, 3.

1. Number of children waiting to be adopted.
2. Ratio of minorities represented by the number of children waiting to be adopted.
3. Number of interracial adoptions in the U.S.

Music is turned up again.

II. MIDDLE

Shot of office door in adoption agency. (very short)

No sound

Full shot of coordinator at her office.

Narration:
"Carolyn Lemieux is the coordinator of the Illinois Adoption Service."

Medium shot of Ms. Lemieux.
Interviewer not seen, except
for the first question.

Interview:

1. What are you looking for in a
   family for a child?
2. What are your policies on
   interracial adoption?
3. Explain the adoption process.
4. Have you had any experience
   with interracial adoption?
   Explain.
5. Would you, as an adoption
   agency, strongly prefer a family
   of the same race as the child?

Fade to full shot of the
Blomgren family cooking
together in the kitchen.

Narration:

"The Blomgrens are an example of a
multicultural family.

"Ake and Gudrun Blomgren
adopted Marie and Christine from
South Korea when the children were
only a few months old."

Shot of Mr. and Mrs. Blomgren in
their living room.

Interview:

1. Why did you adopt two girls who
   are not of the same race as you?
2. How did society react to your
   decision?
3. Have there been any negative
   experiences with having two
   Korean girls when the world
   tends to be racially conscious?

Montage of pictures of Marie and
Christine doing something together.

Go back to shot of
Mr. and Mrs. Blomgren.

4. How have you dealt with your
   daughters natural confusion
   over looking different from you?
5. Have you sensed that people
   have not been comfortable with
   your family because of its racial
   diversity?

Show the family in
the kitchen again.

Fade to shot of the Katz family
doing something together
(such as decorating
the Christmas tree).

Shot of Mr. and Mrs. Katz
in the living room.

Shot of Kim talking on
the phone.

Shot of the family doing
something together.
(See first shot of this interview.)

Fade to shot of Mr. Raphael
working at his office.

6. When have you felt
   uncomfortable with your family
   situation?
7. Have you raised Marie and
   Christine differently considering
   their racial situation?

Narration:
"Kim was born in India. Her parents,
Mr. and Mrs. Katz, adopted Kim
when she was a few months old."

Interview
1. Growing up in racially conscious
   America, was it a difficult step to
   adopt a girl from India?
2. What was the reaction of your
   family and friends?
3. How did you handle the negative
   response?
4. What experiences have you had
   relating to a daughter from a
   different racial group?
5. Do you think that you, as
   individuals, have changed your
   opinions of the racial situation
   in this country because of Kim?
6. Do you think that you, as
   parents, have raised Kim
   differently than biological
   parents have raised their
   children?

Narration:
"Lawrence Raphael is a lawyer and
takes care of many adoption cases."

Close-up shot of Mr. Raphael. Interviewer only seen for the first or second question (depending on how it looks).

Interview:
1. From a legal viewpoint, do you deal with interracial adoption differently than other adoption cases?
2. What are your personal experiences with interracial adoption?

Five-second shot of newspaper article concerning this subject, then go back to shot of Mr. Raphael.

3. Has the legal action by some social workers and lawyers in Minnesota to forbid interracial adoption affected the adoption process?
4. What is your view on that action?

Cut to shot of Ms. Barnett in her office.

Narration:
Ms. Barnett is a child psychiatrist in Chicago.

Close-up shot of Ms. Barnett. Interviewer only seen when asking first question.

Interview:
1. From a psychological viewpoint, how does growing up in a multicultural family affect a child?
2. With no strings attached to the child's biological environment, is it likely that he or she still feels most comfortable with people of his or her own race?
3. How much do the biological strings from a child to a mother impact the mental development of a child?

Cut to shot of Marie Blomgren sitting in her room.

Narration:
"Marie was born in Korea. She was adopted by a white family when she was five months old. Marie does not know anything about her biological background."

Close-up shot of Marie.
Interviewer not seen.

Interview:

1. How does it feel to be part of a multicultural family?
2. How has it affected your life?
3. How did you learn that you were adopted?
4. Do your views on your family situation now differ from when you were little? How?
5. Tell me about experiences relating to your family's interracial situation.

Focus on the ornaments on her wall.

6. Do you feel any attachments to your native country?
7. Have your views of the racial situation here in America been affected by the fact that you are adopted by parents with a different skin color?

Shot of Marie and her parents.

8. How do you respond to people who say that interracial adoption is damaging to the child?

Cut to shot of Kim in her room.

Narration:
"Kimberly Katz is seventeen years old. She was born in India, but came to her American parents, who are white, when she was a few months old."

Close-up of Kim.

Interview:

1. How have you dealt with the controversy of growing up in an interracial family?
2. Tell me some of your experiences relating to your racial background.

Shot of Kim talking on
the phone.

Shot of Kim and her parents.

III. CONCLUSION

Snapshot of needy child.
Shot of the Blomgren family
having dinner.
Snapshot of needy child.
Shot of the Katz family talking.
Picture of child.
(Keep it until the end.)

3. What do you feel when you meet
   an Indian family on the street?
4. What are your views on the
   racial issue, and have they been
   affected by your personal
   background?

Narration:
"The number of homeless and par-
entless children increases while we
battle racism and prejudice. Unfortunately, the children cannot wait
forever. Why let these children become the victims of another American tragedy?"

Music is turned up again.

Animated Ideas

Animation is full of possibilities. It can be a Saturday morning cartoon, a whimsical video of self-operating kitchen gadgets, or a strange, dramatic film of clay figures moving against a painted background.

Whether you want it to look funny, sophisticated, cute, or weird, your animated video will require a special kind of creativity. Reality can be toyed with or ignored completely. You can make a new and very different world and fill it with your own moving visual communication.

While everybody has enough talent to make some type of animated video, some camcorders may not have the best technology to produce a cartoon. The key to technical flexibility is a "flying erase head," a term that you can find in the owner's manual in the section on your camera's specifications. Somewhere among the decibels, hertz, frequency responses, and other technical numbers you'll find a section that describes your camcorder's heads. If it says "flying erase head," which is becoming a more common feature on newer models, you're in luck. If it doesn't, you will still be able to do some types of animation, but you will be much more limited than if you were using a flying erase head.

So just exactly what is this thing that sounds like a flying pencil eraser with a head on it? It is the thing that allows you to start and stop recording without a glitch or a line running distractingly across the frame. In order to start recording, most older camcorders (without flying erase heads) need a running start to get up to speed. But cameras with a flying erase head jump right into action, as the camcorder is already running at full speed. It's kind of like a treadmill running machine. If you were to jump onto a treadmill that was already running at full speed, you would have to run at full speed, too, as soon as you hit the tread. A camcorder without a flying erase head is like an idle treadmill. It takes a few seconds to get up to full speed.

If you don't have an erase head, keep reading anyway, because you can still make your own animation, too.

As I said earlier, there are many types of animation, from drawn cartoons to inanimate objects mysteriously moving. In cartoons such as those with Bugs Bunny, an artist draws thousands of images. Each image might have the same scenery background, but the main character changes slightly. For example imagine Bugs Bunny standing with his arm at his side. To make it appear that Bugs is raising his arm, the cartoon artist produces a series of drawings, each one with Bugs's arm slightly higher than the preceding drawing. It might take as many as twenty-four or more drawings to raise the arm from Bugs's side to above his head.

Today's cartoon producers use computers to minimize much of the tedious drawing work, but in the old days of the 1930s and 1940s, when animation was still evolving into an art form, these drawings were photographed one at a time with the movie camera. When played back, the animated character came to life.

The trick to the whole process was a special motion-picture camera that could record one, two, three, or more frames at a time. Typically, all motion-picture cameras move the film through the shutter (which allows the light to make its image on the film) at thirty frames per second. In other words, to produce ten seconds of a movie, you need three hundred frames of film.

Mounted on a tripod to make sure the background was not moving along with the cartoon characters, the camera would record two frames of film per drawing. Using our example of twenty-four drawings of Bugs moving his hand from his side to above his head, the entire process would consume forty-eight frames (two frames times twenty-four drawings).

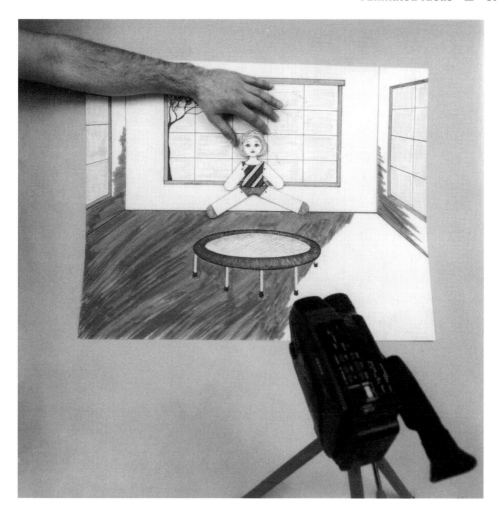

A simple paper doll cutout moved inch by inch on a backdrop drawn on posterboard can serve as an excellent video project.

Unfortunately, it can take a cartoon artist many hours to draw twenty-four drawings, depending on how elaborate they are. And his reward for hours of work will be only two seconds of film time (sometimes called "real time"). If you run out to the kitchen to get a can of pop for ten seconds, you will miss all of that artist's long, hard work.

The problem with today's camcorder is the reduced control you have over time and space. Motion-picture film has sprockets; when you adjust the camera to expose only two frames, it turns the correct amount of sprocket holes for two frames. These are called mechanical actions.

In inexpensive amateur camcorders, this process is more electronic than mechanical. You press the record button and you record a set number of seconds. Since you are counting the seconds yourself and you are not a precision watch, each half-second or one-second push of the record button varies. One time it might be three-quarters of a second. Another time it might be one-half of a second.

If you don't have a flying erase head, there is no way you can cleanly record those two seconds of drawings: it probably takes at least five seconds for the camcorder to warm up and get up to speed!

But don't fear. If you're set on drawing your character and making it move you can still do it in a limited fashion—whether it's raising his arm above his head or making his head fall off and roll along the floor.

Take a tablet of paper and draw your character again and again on a series of pages, making the character move slightly with each drawing. Make sure each drawing is exactly in the same place as the drawing on the previous page of the tablet. You will draw some variance to show motion. In other words, it's OK for Bugs to raise his arm slightly in each drawing, but Bug's body should be the same size and in the same place in each drawing unless, of course, he's dancing or running. Pile the drawings together and fan through the pages using your thumb almost like you would a deck of playing cards. You'll see your character magically move before your eyes. Now turn on your camcorder—whether it has an erase head or not—and record this movement. Point the camera and zoom in so the character fills the frame. We don't want the audience to see the entire tablet of paper. Press record on the camcorder (wait at least ten seconds after pressing record if you don't have a flying erase head), and flip through your drawings. Bingo . . . you've just recorded your first animation.

You can improve on this process if you're handy with a computer and can draw a background for the character. Using a paintbrush computer program, you can draw some type of background. Your background could be trees, mountains, houses, or anything else you want. Print out twenty-four pages of the background on your computer printer, then draw your character doing his movement on each page. Now you'll have a character doing its motion against a static background. Of course you can also draw the background by hand and make black-and-white or color photocopies. This process is sometimes called "filmation."

The possibilities are endless. Your character could run across the page and climb a tree. Of course that might take a whole box of computer paper. If you have a flying erase head, go ahead and begin recording one-half second at a time for each page. It's a lot of work for two seconds, isn't it? So here's an easier way to animate.

Take any object—a pencil, a banana, or your kid brother. With the camcorder on a tripod, record the object for one or two seconds. Then move the object slightly to the left or right. Record another one or two seconds. Keep doing this until the object moves out of the frame. Play your recording back and you'll see you've made some animation. It will look pretty good, too, especially if you have that flying erase head.

The possibilities with this method are endless. You can make a friend move strangely down the sidewalk simply by recording a slight move every one or two seconds. Dub in a locomotive puff-puffing down the track, and your friend will sound like a train as he or she moves down the sidewalk in a herky-jerky motion created by the camcorder animation.

You can also take some putty and make your own character figure. Keep the camcorder aimed on the putty or clay character and record slight movements. This technique is often called "claymation"—a combination of clay figures and animation.

If you want to get really fancy, you can zoom in for a close-up of the character's face in the middle of a movement. If you are showing a clay figure running who suddenly runs into a wall, just before impact, record a close-up of the character's face showing fear. Next, move his putty lips to form a word, such as "ouch!" If your camcorder allows an audio-dubbed soundtrack, you can make the mouth motion spring to audio life.

You can write a script for your clay character to follow. Put in titles and a soundtrack, and you've created animation.

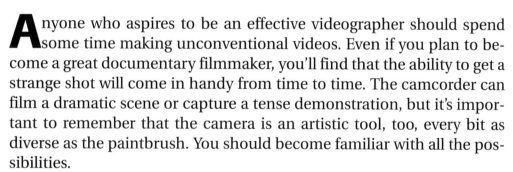

Abstract
Videography

Anyone who aspires to be an effective videographer should spend some time making unconventional videos. Even if you plan to become a great documentary filmmaker, you'll find that the ability to get a strange shot will come in handy from time to time. The camcorder can film a dramatic scene or capture a tense demonstration, but it's important to remember that the camera is an artistic tool, too, every bit as diverse as the paintbrush. You should become familiar with all the possibilities.

Think about how you're using the camera. A close-up of your friend, especially one that fills the frame with his or her face, would be classified as a portrait. You can easily recognize this image as your friend, and a stranger would recognize the image as a human being. But what if you were to get extremely close and show only your friends nostrils? That's right, fill up the entire frame with what will appear to the viewer as two dark holes. Unassuming viewers might mistake the nostrils for two dark, moldy, prehistoric caves, double barrels of a shotgun, twin dark holes in outer space, or whatever triggers their imaginations.

That's the key to abstract videography: triggering the viewer's imagination. Just about anything can became an abstract and unrecognizable image if you get close enough.

Any camcorder can get close enough to an object to give an abstract image. Camcorders with a macro lens are especially good for this technique. A macro lens looks and operates like any camcorder's zoom lens, but it offers one additional feature—the ability to stay in focus when very close to the subject. You can tell if your camcorder has macro capabilities by checking the specifications page of your owner's manual. Many times a camcorder will have the wording "macro" on the lens itself or on the camcorder body. Surprisingly, most camcorders have a macro function, but few people know about it, let alone use it in their videotaping. If you're not sure if your camcorder has a macro function, try filling up the video frame with a coin, such as a quarter. You should be able to fill the frame with only a small border on all sides.

Using the macro function requires a slightly different technique than that required with zoom lenses. In most cases a tripod is necessary, not only to keep the image from shaking, but to keep it in focus. When you're in the macro mode, being in and out of focus can be the difference of only a few millimeters. Macro focusing is very, very precise.

To improve your ability with this technique, practice on that quarter. Next, fill the entire video frame with a penny, and you will notice that it's difficult to keep in focus when holding the camcorder by hand. Try it again using a tripod and you'll see a big difference.

Selecting Your Images

Now that you're a macro expert, find some objects and film extreme close-ups. Try filming the grain of a piece of furniture, the tiny weave of some fabric, or the rough texture of a carpet—even try the bark of a tree outside. The point of a car hubcap where it meets the tire will give you a half-shiny half-black (or matted) texture in the frame. Be careful not to get run over, though!

Next try some close-ups using light to provide contrast. On an indoor object, shine a lamp or a flashlight from the side so that the beam of light is perpendicular to the angle of the lens. Try shining a light source from the side over a plate of grain or other cereal. It might look like the surface of the moon or a sandy beach with rocks.

Try filming a backlit silhouette. Point a light source toward the camcorder. Cover most of the light by placing an object between the light and

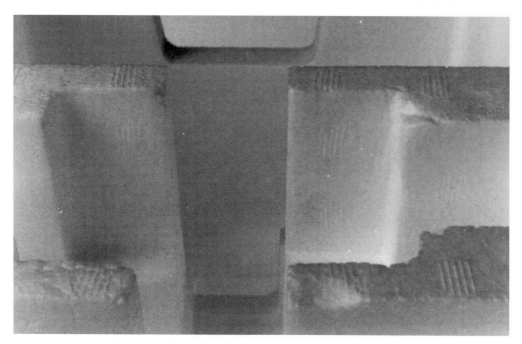

Abstract imagery is easy to do with extreme close-ups or by manually putting your camcorder lens out of focus. These two images are extreme close-ups of Styrofoam packing. The material takes on a different character when seen this close.

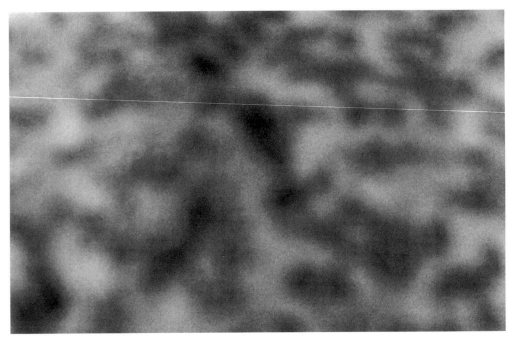

Raindrops on a window? A flurry of locusts? No, this abstract image is a floral pillowcase through a soft-focused camcorder lens.

the camcorder. Be sure to use an item small enough to allow rays of light to spill past the edges of the object.

Next, instead of videotaping the front of an object, try videotaping a long object from its side, but so you can see the top of it. Film the kitchen counter, for example. Place the camcorder level with the plane of the counter. Fill the bottom of the frame with the edge of the kitchen counter, and then fill the top half with the top of the counter. The part of the counter farthest from the lens will look undefined and probably out of focus. That's good, because we're trying to be abstract here. Try changing the proportions of the side and the top of the counter. For example, fill one-quarter of the frame with the side of the counter and three-quarters of the frame with the top. Next try it with the opposite proportions.

Another variation in abstract art is motion. Spin around in a circle while you're recording. Another spinning method is to find something that spins in a circle, such as lazy susan tray. Put the camcorder on the tray and spin it for thirty seconds. This method will provide an unusual perspective on your room. Try spinning your camera in a small room such as a bedroom. Place lights close to each of the four walls and spin

This image is a newspaper's television listing that's slightly out of focus.

the camcorder again. The amount of light and darkness will change very quickly.

Other ways to make abstract imagery include unfocused pictures. I know, I know, we've always stressed keeping pictures finely focused in this book, but now is your big chance for poor technique. We now want out-of-focus pictures. Since you're now an expert camcordist you will find it hard to do something you've been trained to think of as poor technique, but try it! Put the camcorder in manual mode and "unfocus" on an extreme close-up of an item, such as the grain of a piece of wood, a pile of paper clips, a rough-textured wall, or anything else you can find around the house. There are different degrees of focus. One type is called "soft focus." First try fine focusing, then slowly turn the focusing ring of your lens. When the image is slightly out of focus, your picture has a dreamy appearance. Hollywood film directors often use this approach to signal to the viewer that a character is dreaming.

Next go beyond soft focus. Keep unfocusing until objects are unidentifiable. Now you're really creating abstract images. Try this out-of-focus approach from any viewpoint. Try it outdoors and indoors, for close-ups and long shots, and you'll find that, regardless of viewpoint, images become abstract if they are unfocused enough. The camera shouldn't have to be in macro to obtain an abstract effect, although you might want to try out-of-focus macro viewpoints as well.

A particularly interesting out-of-focus image is that of light sources. Any place where there is a collection of small lights, such as tree decorations, store windows, or recessed lights in ceilings, is a good place to try filming. Fill the frame with the unfocused lights. You'll see a potpourri of blurry bright spots that make a very attractive abstract image.

Putting It All Together

After you've collected twenty or thirty images, put them together into a short production. If you preplanned such a production and strung your images together as you were videotaping them, then you're already done. But if you didn't plan it that way and your images need to be cut down by thirty seconds or more and strung together, then try dubbing your camcorder material onto a VCR deck. Make it interesting by varying the lengths of footage devoted to each abstract image. If you have forgotten how to dub onto a VCR deck, turn to chapter 4, "The Video Yearbook."

There is no "proper" way for the images to appear and no "correct" order, but you can employ some of the guidelines used by professional film editors. Pay special attention to pace. How does the pace of the images (the amount of time they appear on screen) affect your audience? Your first images could be longer in length than the last images. Your opening images might stay on the screen about ten seconds each. Gradually make each image a little bit shorter in length until finally the last few pictures are zipping by. This arrangement creates a particular pace, which the viewers may not notice but which affects them subconsciously. The quickening pace of our example creates a mood of increasing excitement, culminating in a climactic finish.

You could also choose the opposite pace for your production. The images then would be brief in the beginning and gradually grow longer toward the end. This pace generate a slower and more relaxed mood in your audience.

Another factor to keep in mind for your edited production is the grouping together of similar images. You could group all rough-textured subjects together versus objects with shiny or slick surfaces. Other grouping patterns might include dark images versus light images, or cool colors

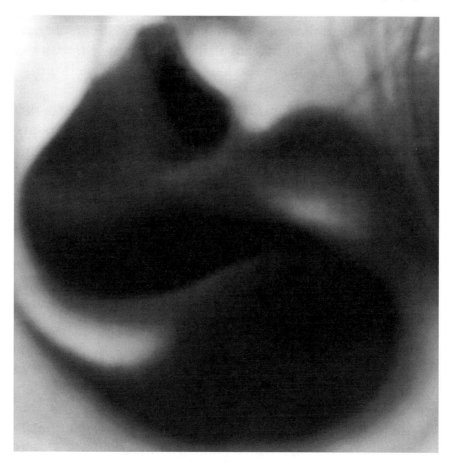

A deep, dark cave? No, this is a human ear.

of blue and green versus hot colors of red and yellow. You could also alternate images of one kind and then another to create an oscillating pattern. It's your choice. Keep in mind that, although they may not seem very crucial, groupings and patterns of images are an important element of any film.

Be sure you haven't stayed with one image for too long in your final production. Ten seconds or less should be long enough for each image, unless it's a movement image such as the spinning or panning movements mentioned earlier. If each image is ten seconds long and you have thirty images compiled, you will have produced a five-minute film. Five minutes is a good length, as audiences, especially those not used to your wild, abstract ideas, may become bored after much longer than that.

One way to enhance your production is to add music. If you have an audio dub button on your camcorder, you can combine music right with the images. If you don't have an audio dub button, you can play back the tape on a television while simultaneously playing music from a stereo or boom box. The music and the videotape won't be synchronized, but they'll appear that way.

Once you've decided on how to add the music to the video, then you must decide what type of music will sound good with the abstract images. There's no right and wrong here, but you'll find abstract music is more complementary to the abstract art images you've created than some more-recognizable music, such as Pearl Jam or Bruce Springsteen songs.

Ah, but where does one find abstract music, and just what exactly is abstract music? Music is usually classified as abstract if it has no melody or easily identifiable tune you can whistle. Several twentieth-century composers, including Igor Stravinsky, Béla Bartók, and Paul Hindemith, wrote many modern-sounding selections. You'll find their record albums or CDs at your local library. Other composers who wrote abstract music are Arnold Schoenberg and Alban Berg. They both took music beyond tonality, that is, their music was not based on a particular set of pitches or musical key (such as the key of B-flat or F). The latter two's music sounds quite different from the music we're used to because of its atonality. If you really want to get crazy with the music for your film, look for compositions by John Cage, which could include anything from people drumming on oven racks to the breaking of a series of glass bottles.

You can make some of your own abstract music if you want just by banging wildly and unpredictably on an electronic keyboard. Take your friend's violin or guitar and try to produce unconventional sounds. Bowing a violin string while moving a finger up and down the string creates an unusual sound. An electric guitar, with the right effects, can create a distorted wall of sound.

Learning to make abstract videos will broaden your options as a videographer. You can combine abstract images with sharp, realistic shots in your other types of video projects. An abstract image can be used to convey the psychological state of a character in a dramatic video or to communicate the mood of a song in a music video.

What is the best thing about abstract videography? It offers completely new and interesting views of everyday objects. A camcorder with a macro lens becomes an invitation to present the common in uncommon ways. What could be a more stimulating exercise for an aspiring filmmaker?

Fade Out: Some Words of Advice

The projects I've suggested in this book are only concepts on paper. It's up to you, the budding filmmaker, to make my basic guidelines come to life on screen. You should use my project ideas not as assignments to be followed precisely, but as kindling for your own creative fires.

Experiment. The exciting thing about making a video is to combine different effects for a compelling result. A surprised audience is an alert audience. Don't be afraid to do the unexpected. After you've experimented, though, examine your final products and decide if they are successful. You want to make videos that work, films that accomplish their goals—whether the goal is to profile a person you know or to sell soap. The idea isn't to show off how many different things you can do with the camera, but to communicate ideas and offer images that keep the viewer interested. But the most important thing is for you to stay interested in your work.

Be a True Student of Film

Try watching movies like you never have before. Instead of following the plot and action like most people, watch the movie with a "how did they do that?" attitude. Try to guess where the camera is in the shot and whether it's moving. Or look at a particular camera angle and determine why the director chose that particular look. You can do this with the music soundtrack—when does it start or stop. Or the effects—is that real fog or a smoke machine on the set.

When you've got your finely tuned eye for detail ready, try viewing some of the movies I've listed below that might offer some ideas on particular chapter projects in this book.

Chapter 2
A Point-and-Shoot Exercise
In *Down and Out in Beverly Hills*, a teenager is making his first home video. When he plays his video back in the last half of the movie, it might give you a good idea of a point-and-shoot exercise.

Chapter 3
Video Letters
If you appear on camera in this chapter or just want to know more about acting in general, try renting Michael Caine's *Acting in Films*.

Chapter 5
Music Videos
Turn on MTV.

Chapter 6
The Art of the Interview
My Dinner with André will show you there's more power in script development and interviewing than in crashing a bunch of cars throughout the movie.

Chapter 7
Commercials
Wouldn't it be nice to see a big assortment of commercials all on one videotape? Well, there is such a thing. There are many videos of award-winning TV commercials. Ask your video store if they have any or can get some for you.

Chapter 8
Comedy

Loads of slapstick comedy routines from old movies can be found on videos at video rental stores. Here are just some of them: The Three Stooges, The Little Rascals, Laurel & Hardy, and The Marx Brothers. Another series that is excellent for its simplicity—it takes place mainly in one room with one camera—is *The Honeymooners*. A good comedy title is *The Best of Soupy Sales*.

Chapter 9
Writing and Videotaping a Script

A few of my favorite scripts, many of which you can order for $25 a piece from Script City, Los Angeles, CA, are *Ghostbusters, Raiders of the Lost Ark*, and *Back to the Future*.

Chapter 10
The Documentary

Two good documentaries are *Roger and Me* and *Woodstock*. Two other documentaries you can rent that show the filmmaking process are *The Making of a Brief History of Time* and *The Making of Gettysburg*.

Chapter 11
Animated Ideas

Just turn on the TV any Saturday morning to see a variety of animation, from the old favorites to the newer computerized versions. A film you can rent is *Academy Award Winners: Animated Short Films*, which will demonstrate many animation styles from all over the world. A title that seems fairly easy to do a spin-off of is *Thomas Gets Tricked and Other Stories*. Thomas, of course, is a toy train.

Chapter 12
Abstract Videography

Few Hollywood films have abstract scenes in them, but see *2001: A Space Odyssey* for unusual abstract images combined with symphonic music.

Inspiration for Rent: Some Films I Recommend

The following films should be available from your local video store or library. These are movies that I think you will find interesting and educational from a filmmaking perspective. Many of them are considered masterpieces; others I've included because they display a particular achievement, such as incredible special effects, breathtaking photography, or perfect comic timing. Of course I could suggest many more films that are worthy of study, but I suspect these will start you off on your pursuit of film history. I hope you will come up with your own inspiring list. I also suggest that you watch some documentaries and silent films, and by all means check out the foreign film section.

Films are listed according to year of release; each title is followed by the director's name. You'll see that I've stopped at 1989. I did this because a great many more films will appear before anyone can make intelligent choices among the films of the current decade.

Watch, learn, and enjoy.

King Kong Merian C. Cooper, Ernest Schoedsack (1933)
Little Women George Cukor (1933)
Gone With the Wind Victor Fleming (1939)
Mr. Smith Goes to Washington Frank Capra (1939)
The Grapes of Wrath John Ford (1940)
Citizen Kane Orson Welles (1941)
Sullivan's Travels Preston Sturges (1941)
The Glass Key Stuart Heisler (1942)
Double Indemnity Billy Wilder (1944)
Lifeboat Alfred Hitchcock (1944)
Gentleman's Agreement Elia Kazan (1947)
Adam's Rib George Cukor (1949)
The Red Badge of Courage John Huston (1951)
Guys and Dolls Joseph L. Mankiewicz (1955)
Around the World in Eighty Days Michael Anderson (1956)
Moby Dick John Huston (1956)
The Ten Commandments Cecil B. DeMille (1956)
Spirit of St. Louis Billy Wilder (1957)
Gigi Vincente Minnelli (1958)
Ben Hur William Wyler (1959)
The Diary of Anne Frank George Stevens (1959)

The Mouse That Roared Jack Arnold (1959)

Some Like It Hot Billy Wilder (1959)

The Longest Day Andrew Marton, Ken Annakin, Bernhard Wicki (1962)

To Kill a Mockingbird Robert Mulligan (1962)

It's a Mad Mad Mad Mad World Stanley Kramer (1963)

The Pink Panther Blake Edwards (1963)

The Birds Alfred Hitchcock (1963)

Father Goose Ralph Nelson (1964)

Good Neighbor Sam David Swift (1964)

My Fair Lady George Cukor (1964)

The Great Race Blake Edwards (1965)

The Odd Couple Gene Saks (1968)

Butch Cassidy and the Sundance Kid George Roy Hill (1969)

Little Big Man Arthur Penn (1970)

The Sting George Roy Hill (1973)

Walking Tall Phil Karlson (1973)

Annie Hall Woody Allen (1977)

Close Encounters of the Third Kind Steven Spielberg (1977)

Star Wars George Lucas (1977)

Days of Heaven Terrence Malick (1978)

Alien Ridley Scott (1979)

The Jerk Carl Reiner (1979)

Chariots of Fire Hugh Hudson (1981)

Raiders of the Lost Ark Steven Spielberg (1981)

Amadeus Milos Forman (1984)

Little Shop of Horrors Frank Oz (1986)

Top Gun Tony Scott (1986)

Big Penny Marshall (1988)

Glory Edward Zwick (1989)

Now go out and enjoy the art of making videos. I look forward to seeing your work when it opens in theaters across the country.

A Sample
Video Script

Ithought a script made into a video seen by hundreds of people would be a good example of how to format a script. This script is by Chicago-based Francis W. Parker School students, Greg Feldman, Courtney Crumley, James Moylan, Jason Burns, and Britney Wislow.

The project was a documentation of the school's various functions. Its intent was to inspire money donations at the private school's annual fund-raising auction. That's why it has the rather unglamorous name, *Auction Video*.

The following is an example of one section of the *Auction Video*, called the "Arts Section." The screenwriters translated their thoughts to video using two methods—as a synopsis and later as a script with video/audio directions.

Paragraphs A, B, C, D, and E each are a synopsis of the five scenes videotaped. Following the synopsis paragraphs are song lyrics that accompany each section as a soundtrack. On page 120, the same five scenes are outlined in a different script format (Visual and Idea Line), where the action is described chronologically for the video production crew to videotape one step or sequence at a time.

You'll notice there are some rapid edits and other scene combinations outlined in this script that would be difficult to accomplish without the editing equipment the school possesses. We don't cover editing (except for in-camera editing and planning) in this book.

In several chapters of this book I talked about grabbing the emotions of the viewer. On paper this script doesn't evoke emotion from the reader. However, once it was videotaped and edited, the music and visuals were very touching. The video evoked the intended response. Many of the attendees of the auction video party were so overwhelmed with it that they donated huge sums of money to the school.

Prose Script for the Arts Section of Auction Video

A. Opening Sequence

The auditorium door is opened by a child's hand, revealing an empty auditorium. The camera moves in, focusing on a spotlight on the stage. A little boy dressed in an oversized Hamlet-Tudor outfit, carrying an oversized sword, walks onto the stage and into the spotlight. "Hamlet" raises his sword and delivers the line, "To be, or not to be." The visual changes to an over-Hamlet's-shoulder shot toward the auditorium. The camera focuses up on the spotlight, which fills the screen. As the screen brightens, the cymbals rise in intensity. The cymbals peak, and the infectious and bouncy guitar licks of the auction song come in.

B. Drama Section

The drama section, approximately one minute and thirty seconds, is a montage of shots from (at least one representative of each) a third grade Thanksgiving play, a Greek play, an eighth grade play, and high-school plays. Mixed in between the different plays are shots of drama classes of all ages, performances, and action shots of all the drama teachers. The lyrics of the song outline the dramatic possibilities at the school. There is a verse and then a chorus, when the drama section ends.

C. Music Section

After the drama section chorus, the music drops down to a simple, funky piano lick. The visual is a shot of a child's hand playing the lick; the shot widens until you can see the child ("Mozart") sitting at the piano, wearing a white wig and a long black cape. The band picks up the piano theme and Mozart continues to play while he furiously conducts an invisible band over the camera's shoulder. When the music section verse begins, the visuals shift to a montage of the school's instrumental and vocal groups, concentrating on classroom and performance shots; mixed in are action shots of all the music teachers. The lyrics highlight the musical possibilities at the school. The section concludes with a chorus.

D. Visual Arts Section

After the music section chorus ends, the band drops out and you see and hear Mozart playing very classical and refined piano chords. The piano continues, while the visuals become "Picassa," a little girl wearing an oversized beret, holding a palette and a paintbrush, gazing at school artwork. Picassa stands before a large white wall, deciding what to paint. As the piano gets louder and more intense, the visuals flash between close-ups of Picassa thinking and shots of Mozart pounding the piano with increasing force. The music builds to a climax, when Picassa takes a bucket of paint and hurls it across the wall. The visual arts section verse begins.

The visuals during the verse and the chorus are a montage of classroom shots, art stills, shots of Picassa painting frenetically, the progress of her huge, luminous creation, and action shots of all the visual arts teachers. The lyrics to the verse and chorus of the visual arts section outline the visual artistic possibilities at the school. The song climaxes in the chorus, and then fades away.

E. Ending Sequence

The visual is a pitch-black auditorium. (There is an audience, but you can't tell until the houselights go on at the end.) A spotlight goes on stage left-center, revealing Picassa standing before her painting. A second spotlight on stage left reveals Mozart sitting at a piano, and he plays a short phrase. A third spotlight reveals Hamlet, who raises his sword and says, "That is the question!" The three children stand frozen for a moment in complete silence, and then the audience begins to applaud. The houselights go on, revealing the audience, who stand up and cheer riotously. The visuals fade out on the smiling faces of Hamlet, Picassa, and Mozart, who are taking bows. The sound fades out with audience applause.

Lyrics for the Arts Section of the Auction Video
Lyrics and Music by Greg Feldman

Drama Section

Said, I want to be an actor
And work on plays all day.
There's so much to do, I'm going to
Rule the eighth grade play.

In third grade we'll act like Pilgrims,
I'll go to Greece in fourth.
With plays in upper school
I'll get a chance to do more and more and

Chorus

I'm going to do all I can do,
And there'll be applause when I'm through,
'Cause my school's got choices that I can pursue.

Music Section

I want to play music
That's why my school's great,
With each little blues lick
I learn to create.

I'm gonna sing in the chorus,
In Chorale and Choir.
There are fabulous teachers
We've got to admire.

Chorus

Our school's music's a part of our lives.
There's room for our talents to thrive
With concerts, recitals, performances live.

Visual Arts Section

Well, I could be a painter
And color vibrant lands.
Or I could work on sculpture,
Get clay all over my hands.

Creating great works of vision
All types and mediums of art
Mom and Dad, good decision,
Sending me here to start.

Chorus

There're so many fun things my way
So much good music to play.
I'll paint, sing, and act till they drag me away.

Visual   # Idea Line

A. Opening Sequence

1. Auditorium door opens to an empty auditorium.

2. Little boy dressed in oversized Hamlet-Tudor outfit, carrying an oversized sword, walks onto stage. Spotlight shines on "Hamlet."

   "To be, or not to be."

3. Over-the-shoulder shot. Focus on spotlight until light from the spotlight becomes blinding.

   Cymbals rise in intensity along with the light. Cymbals peak with raucous guitar sounds. Song begins.

4. Approximately fifteen to thirty seconds.

B. Drama Section

1. Montage of shots

   "I want to be an actor."

   a. Third grade plays

   Lyrics outline dramatic possibilities for all grades.

   b. Greek plays

   c. Eighth grade plays

   d. High-school plays

   e. Drama classes

   f. Performance showcase

2. Approximately one minute and thirty seconds.

   Chorus.

C. Music Section

1. Transition

   Break in the music. Drums keep time on high-hat, while "Mozart" plays a funky piano lick.

   a. Shot of a child's hand playing a piano lick.

b. Shot widens until you see all of "Mozart" sitting at the piano, wearing a long, white wig and a black cape.

Band joins in.

2. Montage of shots

"I want to play music."
Lyrics outline musical opportunities at the school through twelfth grade.

   a. Instrumental groups

   b. Vocal groups

   c. Children singing

   d. Children playing instruments

3. Approximately one minute and thirty seconds.

D. Visual Arts Section

1. Transition

Music turns classical and refined. Guitar, drums, and bass drop out, leaving classical piano.

   a. Mozart playing the first classical piano chords.

   b. Little girl (Picassa) wearing an oversized beret and holding a palette and a paintbrush.

   c. Shots of Picassa looking at high school artwork; her face is contemplative.

   d. Picassa standing in front of a white wall deciding what to paint.

   e. Mozart plucking piano.

   f. Close-up of Picassa.

Music gets rougher; guitar, bass, and drums join in.

   g. Mozart hammering more forcibly.

   h. Picassa

i. Mozart violently and passionately banging on the piano.	Music rises to a crescendo.
j. Picassa picks up bucket of paint and flings it across the wall.	Music climaxes.

2. Montage.   Verse.

   a. Classroom shots   Lyrics outline artistic opportunities at the school through twelfth grade.

   b. Art stills   Final chorus.

   c. Mixed in are shots of Picassa painting frenetically and the progress of her huge, luminous creation.   Music fades away.

3. Approximately one minute and thirty seconds.

E. Ending Sequence

1. Dark auditorium (filled with people, but so dark they can't be seen).

2. Spotlight goes on backstage, revealing Picassa standing frozen in front of her painting.

3. Second spotlight reveals Mozart at the piano; he plays a short phrase.

4. Third spotlight reveals Hamlet.   **"That is the question."**

5. Lights go on in the auditorium, revealing the audience, who stand up and applaud.   Audience applause.

6. Fade out on the smiling faces of Hamlet, Picassa, and Mozart.

Glossary

Abstract An image that is not easily identifiable. In fine art, abstract images are geometric forms or random images (in contrast to more traditional subjects such as landscapes, portraits, or other realistic depictions of objects).

Animation A cartoon or other film that gives motion to inanimate objects.

Auto/Manual Mode In auto mode the camera makes all adjustments automatically; in manual mode the camcorder operator must make all adjustments.

Automatic Focus A function on most camcorders that automatically adjusts the lens for a sharp and clear picture.

Backlight A function on some camcorders that brightens the subject while overexposing the background.

Backlighting Light that comes from behind the subject and makes the subject appear three-dimensional and separate from the background.

Claymation Animation that is produced from clay figures.

Close-Up A camcorder view that shows only the subject's face.

Conflict A challenge or problem that confronts the main characters in a drama. Typically, the main character spends much of the drama trying to solve the problem.

Cue Cards Large cards on which the dialogue of the video is printed. If actors forget their lines they can refer to the cue cards, which are usually displayed near the camera.

Depth of Field The focal range of a scene from foreground to background. A deep depth of field has both the background and the foreground in focus—usually used when the scene is very well lit such as in direct sunlight. A shallow depth of field—usually used when the scene is poorly lit—leaves the background out of focus when the foreground is in focus.

Dew Indicator A warning signal most camcorders have that is usually seen through the viewfinder and indicates if there is too much moisture in the camcorder. If the moisture content becomes too high the camcorder will shut down.

Dialogue What the actors say to each other.

Diffused Light Light that is shone indirectly at the video subject. For diffused light, the light is bounced off something white, such as a posterboard, a wall, or an umbrella. Diffused light is softer than direct light and offers less harshness and contrast.

Dolly A device on wheels that allows the camcorder to move without too much bouncing or bumping. Many times it is a tripod on wheels. On professional video dollies, the wheels are made to roll on a set of tracks, much like a train, to reduce bouncing even more. The tracks can be laid in the direction the camera is to be moved.

Dry Acoustics When only a small amount of echo or reverberation is produced in a room or space. A room that soaks up sound with rugs and other soft surfaces such as sofas and pillows provides dry acoustics. In a room with mostly hard surfaces such as wood flooring and hard, flat-surfaced furniture the sound bounces off the walls and floor, producing live acoustics. Speech is more audible in a dry room.

Dubbing Substituting an alternate video or audio track for the track that was recorded live.

Duplicate To make a copy of a videotape. A duplicate is sometimes referred to as a dub.

Fade-In A gradual change in the picture from a blank screen to a full image. Many camcorders offer fade-in control as an accessory.

Fade-Out The opposite of fade-in; a gradual change from full picture to a blank screen.

Feedback An electronic process in audio equipment that produces a piercing, squealing sound. Usually a monitor will feedback when the volume is turned up and a camcorder is feeding a live signal through it.

Flying Erase Head A feature in some camcorders that eliminates glitches when the camcorder begins recording because no motor warm-up time is required. With a flying erase head a series of glitchless recordings can be made simply by engaging and disengaging the record button.

Format The operating system of a camcorder. Today there are two main operating formats—8mm and VHS. Neither format is compatible with the other; therefore, tapes made on one format are unplayable on the other.

Framing How a shot is composed in the viewfinder; different framings include the long shot, the medium shot, and the close-up.

Frontlighting Light that comes from behind the camcorder and makes the subject very bright.

Genre A categorization of an art form that identifies it and separates it from other art forms. For example Westerns, comedies, and science-fiction films are three different genres within the classification "motion pictures."

Hair light A light that creates a sheen on the subject's hair, separating him or her from the background. The hairlight is placed out of sight of the camera.

Handheld When the camcorder is held with the hands or on one's shoulder without the use of a supporting device such as a tripod.

Improvise To make something up on the spur of the moment. In videography, it usually refers to actors inventing their own dialogue rather than using a prewritten script.

Iris Like the iris of the human eye, the camcorder's iris determines and controls the amount of light that enters the camcorder.

Jack A hole in a camcorder where a plug is inserted to connect it to another piece of equipment, such as a microphone or a VCR.

Jingle A musical song, with lyrics, that promotes a product. Jingles appear on TV and in radio commercials.

Karaoke Music Prerecorded music of popular songs without the lead vocals.

Lavaliere A very small microphone that clips onto the lapel or collar of the subject's clothing.

Lens Cap A cap that fits on the lens to protect it from scratching and dust.

Lip-Synching Moving the lips as if singing the lyrics to a song but without producing any vocal sound.

Long Shot A camcorder view that shows the subject and its surroundings.

Low Light Indicator A warning light or word that appears on the viewfinder screen to tell the camcorder operator that not enough ambient light is available to make a videotape with good resolution.

Macro A function available on some camcorder lenses that allows smaller objects, such as a penny or pencil tip, to be recorded in focus as a large object filling the entire screen.

Manual In manual mode, all functions are adjusted by hand without any of the camcorder's automatic functions; usually applied to focusing and white balance.

Master The original version of a videotape, sometimes called a source, from which duplicates can be made.

Mechanical Process controlled by a machine with moving parts. Today, many mechanical functions are being replaced by digital functions—processes controlled by electricity and computers.

Medium Shot A camcorder view of the subject from the waist to just above the head.

Microphone, External A microphone is usually purchased separately from the camcorder. It usually has a long cable allowing the user to bring the microphone closer to the subject while keeping the camcorder at a distance.

Microphone, On–Camera The microphone that comes as standard equipment on camcorders. Some on-camera microphones can be disconnected from the camcorder, while others are stationary and can't be removed.

Monitor A television that is used to watch a videotape.

Nicad Battery The most popular type of camcorder battery. "Nicad" stands for nickel cadmium—the two principal elements used inside the battery. Nicad batteries are the best type of battery for recharging, as they hold a charge the longest.

Patch Cord A cable that connects two pieces of equipment, such as a camcorder and a VCR.

Plot The story of a dramatic presentation. Plots typically have a beginning, a middle, and an end.

Real Time The actual time it took for something to happen versus the time in an edited version. Production of a scene is usually longer than the final running time.

Record (1) To put an image on film or a sound on tape. (2) The VCR that makes a duplicate from a master or source tape.

Record Button The button that causes the camcorder to begin recording.

Resolution The clarity of the video picture. Light, tape speed, and other factors affect picture resolution.

Reverberation Another term for echo.

Safety Tab A small square plastic piece on all VHS videocassettes, which, when removed, will not allow the cassette to be recorded on. On other types of cassettes, such as 8mm, the safety tab is in the form of a red door that slides back and forth to disable the cassette.

Soft Focus A slightly out-of-focus image in which the subject edges are not clear or defined.

Source (1) The original version of a videotape, sometimes called a master. (2) The VCR in which the master is played to make a duplicate on a record VCR.

SP, LP, and SLP The three speeds of a camcorder and/or VCR. They stand for short play, long play, and super long play. At SP, LP, and SLP, a videotape on a VCR will run for a maximum of two hours, four hours, or six hours, respectively. The SP length on camcorders, however, can vary anywhere from twenty minutes to two hours depending on the format (S-VHS, 8mm, VHS-C, etc.). All camcorders have an SP speed. Some equipment has EP as another speed choice. EP stands for extra play and indicates a running time that's twice the length of the short play.

Storyboard The plot of a videotape drawn in sequential, detailed pictures.

Synopsis A summary or a condensed version of a longer story.

Tape Transport The part of the camcorder that holds the videotape and that pushes outward when you press the eject button.

Telephoto A function of the zoom lens on all camcorders that provides an enlarged view with a long focal length.

Tripod A device with three legs that supports a camera and provides smoother shooting than handheld recordings.

Troubleshooting A methodical process of checking to determine why something isn't operating correctly.

Videographer A person who makes videotape productions.

Video Presence How actors portray themselves on a videotape.

Viewfinder The camcorder's viewing screen. Many of today's camcorder viewfinders allow you to play back your videotape immediately.

White Balance An adjustment on a camcorder that automatically ensures that videotaped colors are exactly the same shades as the real colors they recorded.

Wide Angle A function of the zoom lens on all camcorders that provides the maximum viewing area within a short focal length.

About the Author

John Parris Frantz is a videographer, photographer, video teacher and consultant, and a regular contributor to *Camcorder* magazine. He lives in Chicago.

ZIGGURAT BOOKS
FROM CHICAGO REVIEW PRESS

Ziggurat A temple of the ancient Assyrians and Babylonians, having the form of a terraced pyramid of successively receding stories. Assyrian *ziqquratu*, summit, mountain top, from *zaqaru*, to be high.
—*American Heritage Dictionary of the English Language*

Ziggurat Books are project books for talented young people of middle- and high-school age, ten or eleven and up. Many are science or technology oriented; others involve literature or the fine and applied arts. All emphasize a hands-on, experimental approach to adult disciplines such as physics, astronomy, the graphic arts, architecture, and creative writing.

Ziggurat Books give students a taste of a wide variety of adult professions. They provide innovative, challenging material for science and art fairs, class and individual school projects. Most important, they enable young people to explore their talents as they experience the effort and the excitement of creative work.

These books are available through your local bookstore or directly from Independent Publishers Group, 814 North Franklin Street,
Chicago, Illinois, 60610, 1-800-888-4741.
Visa and MasterCard accepted.

**The Art of Construction:
Projects and Principles for
Beginning Engineers and
Architects**
by Mario Salvadori
ISBN 1-55652-080-8
156 pages, paper, $9.95

**The Art & Craft of
Graphic Design:
Techniques and Projects**
by Julia Dunlop and
Patricia Schreiber
ISBN 1-55652-229-0
200 pages, paper, $14.95

**The Art of the Handmade Book:
Designing, Decorating, and
Binding One-of-a-Kind Books**
by Flora Fennimore
ISBN 1-55652-146-4
144 pages, paper, $11.95

**Exploring the Sky: Projects for
Beginning Astronomers**
Revised Edition
by Richard Moeschl
ISBN 1-55652-160-X
428 pages, paper, $14.95

**Faraday's Chemical
History of a Candle:
Twenty-Two Experiments
and Six Classic Lectures**
by Michael Faraday
ISBN 1-55652-035-2
136 pages, paper, $9.95

**Real Toads in Imaginary Gardens:
Suggestions and Starting Points
for Young Creative Writers**
by Stephen Phillip Policoff
and Jeffrey Skinner
ISBN 1-55652-137-5
192 pages, paper, $11.95

**Seeing for Yourself:
Techniques and Projects for
Beginning Photographers**
by Roger Gleason
ISBN 1-55652-159-6
200 pages, paper, $14.95

**The Spark in the Stone:
Skills and Projects from the
Native American Tradition**
by Peter Goodchild
ISBN 1-55652-102-2
138 pages, paper, $11.95

CHICAGO
REVIEW
PRESS